CRISIS:
Mine's Cancer.
What's Yours?

Falling to Pieces in a Crisis Was Not an Option for Me

ELLEN HARBIN

WESTBOW°
P R E S S
A DIVISION OF THOMAS NELSON
& ZONDERVAN

Cover Design by: Jenny Johnson, JenRose Design
Author Photo by: Erin Wetzel; StudioE Photography, Imlay City, MI
Edited by: Christine Harbin

Scripture taken from the King James Version of the Bible.

Scriptures taken from the Holy Bible, New International Version®, NIV®. Copyright © 1973, 1978, 1984, 2011 by Biblica, Inc.™ Used by permission of Zondervan. All rights reserved worldwide. www.zondervan.com The "NIV" and "New International Version" are trademarks registered in the United States Patent and Trademark Office by Biblica, Inc.™ All rights reserved.

All Scripture quotations in this publications are from **The Message**. Copyright (c) by Eugene H. Peterson 1993, 1994, 1995, 1996, 2000, 2001, 2002. Used by permission of NavPress Publishing Group.

WestBow Press books may be ordered through booksellers or by contacting:

WestBow Press
A Division of Thomas Nelson & Zondervan
1663 Liberty Drive
Bloomington, IN 47403
www.westbowpress.com
1 (866) 928-1240

ISBN: 978-1-4908-4247-9 (sc)
ISBN: 978-1-4908-4248-6 (hc)
ISBN: 978-1-4908-4249-3 (e)

Library of Congress Control Number: 2014911611

Printed in the United States of America.

WestBow Press rev. date: 7/28/2014

Contents

Dedication

This book is dedicated to Bette Willard who, like Anna in Luke 2:37-38, worships God night and day and speaks to everyone about Jesus.

Bette, when I was a young girl you came to my house to lead Backyard Bible Studies for the children in my neighborhood. You were one of my Sunday School teachers. I listened to you give public testimonies about what God was doing in your life when I was a child, a teenager, a young adult and each testimony left an impact on me. You prayed for my husband regarding his call to pastoral ministry before he or I had even heard that call from God. You've prayed for my family for years. You are an example of how to live out the marriage vows as you loved your sweet Roy, in life and since his death. You volunteered to teach and pour into a small group of newly married wives, which I was one, around your dining room table, armed only with the Word of God. You have a passionate, current, thriving, abundant love relationship with Jesus Christ that is contagious. You have been a constant source of Godly wisdom in my life. You have been a role model of how to not fall to pieces through life's challenges and crises. God has used you to challenge me to do things in the Name of Jesus that I never dreamed possible.

I admire many women. I have what are referred to as "heroes" in my life. But, Bette, you are at the top of the list. You have always been a woman warrior for Jesus who I admire, respect and want to emulate.

I love you, Bette Willard, and am greatly blessed to call you friend and sister-in-the-Lord.

Introduction

Ellen Harbin, author

"If you fall to pieces in a crisis there wasn't much to you in the first place."

(Proverbs 24:10, The Message)

"You have cancer."

Those words were the beginning of a journey, a crisis, I never anticipated taking.

Cancer was not my first crisis in life. Nor will it be my last. There have been many. There will be more. Yet it was my cancer that God used to show me how to accept a crisis, how to face a crisis, and how to deal with a crisis. This book is about what I learned on that journey. This book is about what God taught me before, during, and after my crisis.

If you are reading this book, you have either had a crisis, are in the midst of a crisis, or will one day experience a crisis. Some of you may think your crisis isn't as bad as cancer so this book won't be applicable to your life. Some of you may have dealt with or are living a crisis right now that to you seems far more difficult than cancer. It isn't my desire to rank crises. I won't do that. It's impossible to do that. God doesn't do that.

"If you fall to pieces in a crisis there wasn't much to you in the first place" (Proverbs 24:10 The Message). It's a phrase God chose to have in His Word. He made it up and then He had it written down in His Holy Word, His communication to His children. He desires that His followers would know Him deeper each day. Reading His Word allows that. Obeying His Word allows that.

God decided to have Proverbs 24:10 be a nugget for His children to chew on, to apply to their lives. God uses the word 'crisis' for a reason. He didn't get specific with what the crisis may be. He didn't leave the phrase as a fill-in-the-blank sentence. Otherwise Proverbs 24:10 would look like this:

"If you fall to pieces in a crisis, like _____, then there wasn't much to you in the first place"

He knew His children, His followers, couldn't handle that option very well. A crisis can be translated as trouble, distress, affliction, adversity, tribulation, torment, plague, difficulty; many things could be defined or described as a crisis. God doesn't say the crisis is small or large or medium sized; He doesn't refer to this particular crisis here in Proverbs as anything specific; He simply says if a crisis causes you to fall to pieces your strength may be small, tight, narrow; or as The Message version of the Bible so adequately says, *"...there wasn't much to you in the first place"*.

If God were to have listed all the possible crises people could experience, the list would be pages long - He wouldn't leave anything out. Each individual person's crisis is just that, it's theirs. Each of us has trouble. Each of us has distress. Your affliction is different than my tribulation. My difficulty is not your torment. My crisis is mine; your crisis is yours.

Our crises may be different, but we have the same God. It is my prayer that by reading this book you will be encouraged, inspired, and influenced by what God has taught me before, during, and after my crisis.

"You have cancer" are powerful words. They were hard-to-swallow words. They were life-altering words.

My life was busy. Everything fit neatly into my calendar. I had no room for a crisis. I did not volunteer for one.

Crisis is defined as a dramatic emotional or circumstantial upheaval in a person's life. Cancer definitely caused an upheaval in my life. It showed up without notice or permission and shook everything up.

I had plans. Big plans. Good plans. Life-altering, powerful plans when cancer dumped into my life in a dramatically emotional way. This crisis wasn't a part of any of those plans. When the words "you have cancer" interrupted our lives my husband and I had recently made the decision to adopt more children and we were at the final stage of the adoption process when the upheaval showed up. "What?" and "How could this be?" were our thoughts. We just knew God had led us to adopt; it was His idea planted in our hearts. Only God could cause two people, with an empty nest on the horizon, to consider adopting two younger children. We just knew that God had caused six people (2 parents + their 4 biological children) to all be on the same page, to all be so excited, to be so ready for His plan, His idea. When those three words, those life-altering words came tumbling to my ears causing upheaval, I wondered "how did we hear that wrong? We thought for sure that God had called us to adopt... but now this? Cancer? How is that a part of His plan?" To me, this just didn't make sense.

When something falls, it breaks. In a popular nursery rhyme, Humpty Dumpty fell. Humpty Dumpty breaks. That's because Humpty was Dumb-ty. We've been taught that Humpty is an egg. When a large egg is on top of a tall wall, it will roll off the edge and sustain a great fall. And then it will break. It's an egg. Eggs, when rolled off a tall edge of a wall, break. That's rather *dumb*, I say.

I felt like I was teetering on an edge when those three words came rolling into my life. I knew I didn't want to imitate Mr. Dumb-ty

- I didn't want to fall and break. A crisis has the ability to push us to the edge. A crisis has the ability to cause us to fall off the edge, the wall. I had no control over my crisis but I had all control over how I was going to approach, deal with, and face this crisis.

God's Word resonated within me. *If you fall to pieces in a crisis there wasn't much to you in the first place.* Yes. That is straight out of God's Word, from The Message translation of the Bible. I prefer to read, study, and teach from the New International Version (NIV) of the Bible, however, I use many other versions and translations as I study. The NIV says it this way, "If you falter in times of trouble how small is your strength?"

How did I want to face this crisis? Well, I knew one thing: though I had a crisis, it never had me. And because of that, I knew I didn't want the crisis to be the focus.

Humpty Dumb-ty fell, he broke, and all the focus was on how he couldn't be put back together again. I didn't want my crisis to have me in a broken pile, like Mr. Dumpty.

Humpty lay in a pile of broken pieces. All the king's men just stared at the pieces. They gazed at the brokenness. It's all they could do. They couldn't put Humpty together again. Well, perhaps if they had gone to the King, rather than just his men, they would have found a solution of how he could have been made whole again. That's what happens when we allow Christ, the King of kings and Lord of lords, to be the Master of our crises.

This book is about my crisis; it's my story. Along with my story, you will read parts of God's Story. Mixed in with my journey are stories of people from the Bible who are role models to me, examples of how to not fall to pieces in a crisis. As a Bible Study writer/teacher and conference/retreat speaker I love to use people in God's Word to apply to our current, everyday situations; whether they are experiencing crises or not. They teach me. They point me in the right direction. They lead me right to The Christ.

That's my desire with this book, that you will be led to The Christ as you read about how my Lord taught me how to not fall to pieces in a crisis.

Jesus, thank You for being our ultimate example as You walked in obedience all the way to Your crisis, to the cross, so that we could be in relationship with our Father, God, through Your death. You didn't stay dead for long. You rose from the dead. Thank You, Lord, that the same power that raised Christ from the dead is the same power that resides in each child of Yours and makes it possible for us to not fall to pieces. May each person reading this book be encouraged by You, Holy Spirit, and may they be led to You, the Christ. May the words in this book and the meditation of all our hearts be acceptable to You, O Lord, my Rock and My Redeemer.
In Jesus' Name, Amen.

CHAPTER 1

Prior to the Crisis

It was a hot summer day, early in the evening of 2008. Kevin, my husband, and I were sitting in the den, reading side-by-side, enjoying the sounds of our four teenaged kids and approximately six of their friends who were in the family room making plans for the evening. We heard, "let's go get ice cream!" and out the door they went. Our house went from crazy loud to silence in a matter of seconds. Kevin and I looked at each other and our first thoughts weren't what most would guess…"I don't like how quiet it just got." As parents approaching an empty nest, we should have relished the quiet, but it left us wanting something more.

We didn't realize it at that moment but God was stirring in us an awakening. He was preparing our hearts for His plan. His plan? Adoption. He used that quiet moment to speak rather loudly to us; to awaken His plan in our life. And that wasn't the only time He worked in such a way. He woke us up many times to this particular plan. He pricked our hearts often in ways that opened our eyes to His plan.

For instance, not long after that, I was speaking as part of a women's retreat and during one of the meals I happened to sit next to a woman whose family had recently adopted children. She and her husband had raised biological children and then adopted two elementary aged children…right at the time when empty-nest was in sight.

Coincidence? No way. Like a symphony directed by a seasoned conductor, God orchestrated that moment for me. That is only one example of many other similar moments where God kept the adoption idea stirring, the spark ablaze in our hearts.

It was about February of 2009 when Kevin and I began to research adoption and we started looking at overseas adoptions. After an exhaustive search we realized the financial commitment was not an option for us. I remember this next conversation as if it were yesterday. In my mind's eye I see us in the family room, I see where we're each sitting and I can almost hear Kevin's voice as he says so matter-of-factly, "Hey Babe, how would you feel about checking out the Methodist Children's Home Society (MCHS) and seeing what they have to say about adopting children through the foster system in our state?" Well, wasn't he so smart? Of course!

MCHS has been a fixture in the area/community I was raised in, and being raised in the United Methodist denomination I knew of MCHS. Years earlier it served as an orphanage and residential home for children. It later became what it is today, a foster & adoption agency.

I immediately found the organization's website, located the 'adopt' link and began reading. We were primarily interested in the cost of this method, since that was the piece that stopped us from pursuing overseas adoption. I clicked on the 'adopt' link and found: **HOW MUCH WILL IT COST?** This is what we read, "Adopting a child is free; however, there is a county court filing fee which should not exceed $250."

WHAT?!?!?! We felt like we needed to do one of those rub-your-eyes-to-make-sure-you-read-it-right things. Really? $250? Tops? You've got to be kidding! We had "adopted" a dog from the local shelter and even that required a fee. Surely I had read that wrong. We sat in bewilderment, a confusing tangle of emotions. Yet, excitement ruled and so began our journey.

2

After reading that, in essence, there is no financial obligation to adopting children through the foster system we knew we had zero roadblocks. Nothing stood in our way.

Just a few months later, in August, we chose MCHS to be our adoption agency. We found out that our state, Michigan, requires 24 hours of helpful teaching, training, and orientation for those interested in adopting through this avenue, in the form of three eight hour sessions held on consecutive Saturdays. Being in full-time ministry, having two kids in college, and two in high school made us a busy family. Our calendars rarely had three available Saturdays in a row with no prior commitments. However, we serve a God who had a plan and apparently He already had our calendar in His capable hands because the next available training dates were in September and for three Saturdays in a row our calendars were empty. With no obstacles, Kevin and I attended all trainings.

After completing the trainings and filling out a variety of initial paperwork, we were assigned a case worker and began the home study part of the adoption process. (This was just another way we knew God was in control of this process. The case worker assigned to us was Pam, a woman who is still a part of our lives today. We love her. You'll read more about Pam later.)

A home study is a highly involved, multi-step, detailed study of our family. It involves things like the case worker coming to our house for in-home evaluations and inspections, face-to-face interviews, local police clearance, FBI fingerprinting, collection of financial data, biographical information, social histories, detailed character references and medical physicals.

To accomplish the required physicals, I had two back-to-back doctor's appointments. I went to my family doctor and the gynecologist, one for a general physical and the other for the often dreaded/avoided ladies physical. Both told me I was the picture of health.

Two weeks later everything changed. Two weeks later I was no longer that picture of health.

I woke up one morning at the end of October bleeding heavily. This had never happened to me before. I had a decision to make. I could have just waited a few days or weeks to see if it stopped; after all, being forty five at that time, it was possible for me to be premenopausal. However, I was still quite regular in my monthly periods and this mid-cycle bleeding caused me to make a decision. I called my gynecologist that morning.

He also had a decision to make. He could have said, "Since I just saw you 2 weeks ago and everything was fine, let's give this some time and see what happens." But he didn't say that. Instead, he said, "Well, that's not good. Let's have you come in for an ultrasound and see what's going on." That afternoon I was in his office having an internal ultrasound of my uterus. The results were a 'thickening of the uterine lining.' The doctor called for further testing.

Two weeks later, the middle of November 2009, the bleeding subsided. We could have decided to stop the testing then; after all, the bleeding had stopped. But I went for the further testing, a procedure referred to as a hysteroscopy. This allows the doctor to detect and biopsy anything abnormal. During the test my doctor said he noticed something "fluffy" that required him to take a sample, as well as a sample of the uterine lining. He told me he didn't think there was anything to worry about but we may have to discuss removing my uterus at some point in the near future. Since it was a week before Thanksgiving he told me to come back in two weeks to discuss the results of the biopsy.

While all this was happening, I was in the middle of teaching a ten-week Bible study that I had written called "Women Warriors: Those who chose to do the right thing no matter what." When this 'surprise attack' came, when this crisis loomed, I was teaching week nine of this ten-week study. The class focused on some obscure and unpopular women who chose to do the right thing in the midst of a crisis. It was during my preparation for this study that God revealed Proverbs 24:10 (The Message) to me. "If you fall to pieces in a crisis, there wasn't much to you in the first place."

For weeks I had studied and then taught about women who faced trying times, trouble, affliction, distress; women who encountered bad news, women who were in crisis. For weeks I had quoted Proverbs 24:10 and applied it to each woman warrior as she faced her particular crisis. For weeks I studied, wrote, and taught about women in God's Word who chose to do the right thing *no matter what!*

Throughout the chapters of this book, you'll read my story, but you'll also meet some women from God's Word who teach us how they handled their crises.

Prior to my crisis God's Word spoke directly to me, "If you fall to pieces in a crisis, there wasn't much to you on the first place."

CHAPTER 2

Preparation Before the Crisis

It was drilled into my spirit, cemented into my soul, that the time to prepare for a crisis is not when faced with it, or even in the middle of it, but rather well in advance. As I studied, wrote, and taught about the women who chose to do the right thing no matter what, I had no clue that I was about to be faced with my own crisis. I wasn't expecting it. I didn't stand in line and volunteer for a medical crisis. I didn't have it on my calendar. But preparing for a crisis and being prepared for one, should it ever come, are two different thoughts.

Preparing for a crisis is assuming one will come; it's like living in a state of anticipation, anxious about what tomorrow may bring. God's Word has something to say about being anxious for tomorrow. Philippians 4:6 (NIV) says, "Do not be anxious about anything..." I love how God's Word is straight forward. It's not difficult to understand. *Do not be anxious.* That's pretty easy to understand. Where it gets difficult or challenging is deciding if we'll obey His Word or not.

I wasn't focused on *when* a crisis would come I was focused on studying God's Word and teaching it to women. That's an act of being prepared for me. Every lesson He teaches me as I study His Word is preparation for *no matter what*, not being focused on when a crisis is coming, but being prepared to not fall to pieces should a crisis come.

I have been studying and writing Bible Studies for years and the phrase 'fear of the Lord' seems to come up often. I was intrigued with that phrase, that concept, that thought. What does it really mean to 'fear the Lord'? God's Word has the answer.

Deuteronomy 10:12-13 (NIV)

> [12] "And now, Israel, what does the Lord your God ask of you but to **fear the Lord** your God, to walk in obedience to him, to love him, to serve the Lord your God with all your heart and with all your soul, [13] and to observe the Lord's commands and decrees that I am giving you today for your own good?"

I have never found it very easy to memorize Scripture. I love when a song is written using passages, words, or phrases from the Bible; that's one way I can memorize God's Word. I desperately desired to know these two verses from Deuteronomy. I even took liberties and swapped my name for 'Israel'. "And now, *Ellen*, what does the Lord ask of you but to **fear the Lord** your God..." I thought long and hard, I took time to reflect, to chew on, what comes next in those verses.

This passage was first revealed to me as I was studying the second book of the Bible, Exodus. In the first chapter we're introduced to a couple of gutsy women. I like gutsy women. These are two of those Women Warriors I referred to earlier; women who do the right thing no matter what. How these two women, from God's Word, respond to their crisis encouraged me when my crisis exploded into my life. In Exodus 1:15 (NIV) we meet Shiphrah & Puah. Their names have significant meaning.

Shiphrah means beauty.
Puah means splendor.

After digging in deep to this particular story we can see how each of their names meaning reaches to the very core of who they are and how they desired to be known and remembered; for how they shined for their Lord in the face of adversity. Or said differently; how they didn't fall to pieces in a crisis. These gutsy women were Israelites. God had chosen to be in a special, covenant relationship with this particular nation.

The entire nation of Israel had been in bondage to Egypt. How did they arrive in Egypt? Well, it's a long story. To sum it up Jacob (also called Israel) moved his family to Egypt because the land Jacob was living in had a famine and Egypt had plenty of resources. About 70 people in all traveled to Egypt. The plan was to stay only as long as the famine lasted.

But they stayed longer.
About 400 years longer.

By this time the nation of Israel had grown. A lot. They had multiplied to over a million people. "Wow", you may be thinking, "That's a lot of growth." However, when God established His covenant with these people He made some "I will" statements, promises. One of those "I wills" was that Israel would become a great nation.

God told Jacob, his daddy Isaac, and his grandpa Abraham the same thing numerous times, "you will be fruitful and multiply greatly." God had said, "*I will* make you fruitful..." And they were. Because God said so. Covenant God keeps His Word. Egypt was threatened by how fast this nation of people was growing inside their nation. The Pharaoh, the king in Egypt, saw a potential problem so he came up with a plan to stop their growth.

Plan #1 - Slavery

The land of Egypt became a house of bondage to the Hebrew people (also known as Israelites). They had been forced to work hard and live in horrific conditions. The Pharaoh dealt shrewdly with them. His intention was to break their spirits, cause poor physical

8

health, potentially shorten their life spans, make conception and child bearing difficult, and hinder or even halt the worship of their God.

Yet Exodus 1:12 (NIV) says, "But the more they were oppressed, the more they multiplied and spread."

For a Christian who desires to focus on the preparation before the crisis, this is a crucial point. The more oppressed, abused, distressed, enslaved, and helpless they were, they grew in number. The same can be true for you. You, too, can grow even when oppressed, helpless, and distressed; in crisis. That comes through the preparation. Know ahead of time where you stand. Know ahead of time that nothing stands in the way of your growth in your relationship with Jesus; *not even a crisis*. The right time to draw your line is before the crisis comes and say, "No matter what, I will not fall to pieces."

Shiphrah and Puah did this. They drew their lines. These two women knew how they would respond before their crisis reared its ugly head.

Plan #1 failed. Pharaoh didn't like that.

Plan #2 - Murder Babies

Exodus 1:16 (NIV) Pharaoh says to the midwives, Shiphrah and Puah, "When you help the Hebrew women in childbirth and help them on the delivery stool, if it is a boy, kill him; but if it is a girl, let her live."

Shiphrah and Puah didn't *react* to the crisis, they *acted* out of the fact that they had already prepared before the crisis. How did they prepare? Exodus 1:17 (NIV) gives the answer to that question. Exodus 1:17 is the key to preparing before a crisis comes. Exodus 1:17 says, "The midwives, however, **FEARED GOD** and did not do what the king of Egypt told them to do."

The midwives feared God.

Shiphrah and Puah, beauty and splendor, feared God.
That's beautiful and that's splendid!

To fear the Lord is not to be afraid of Him. This fear refers to an awe of who God is and a reverence to His character, to His ways. The midwives stood in awe of their God, they adored, admired, and were loyal to their God and to His Laws. They were committed to His ways. These women were more concerned with doing the right thing. They acted and responded the way God would expect from those who fear Him.

These two women were more afraid of disobeying their God, putting their covenant relationship with Him in jeopardy, rather than listen to the Pharaoh and obey his mandates.

Disobeying the Pharaoh came with great consequence. Death. They knew what was at stake and they were willing to face the king's penalty rather than disobey their God. These women stood in awe of their God.

These two women were prepared *before* their crisis came.
These two women chose to live in the **FEAR of the LORD**.

God had an assignment for these two women, a God-sized, God-given assignment and their preparation for this assignment came well before the actual assignment. Their hearts, the way they chose to live their very lives, were determined before their assignment was given. Yes, these two women were prepared for their particular crisis before it came.

Deuteronomy 10:12-13 gives us the steps necessary to follow the same plan as these two women. This passage teaches us to be prepared for whatever crisis or God-sized assignment that comes our way.

"What does the Lord ask of you but to **fear the Lord** your God..."

- Walk in all His ways
- Love Him
- Serve Him
- Observe His commands

As I said, memorization isn't one of my strengths. So God gave me an acronym to remember His mandate, to live this decree, His way:

S.L.O.W.

Serve God
Love God
Observe His commands
Walk in all His ways

God has a way of reminding His children of the promises, the prayers, and the life changes they have made in His Name. He will remind us of the commitments we've vowed and pledged. He'll bring them to memory. If necessary, He'll rewrite them on our hearts.

He surely did with me. I'll give you a glimpse into one of these moments when God found it necessary to rewrite on my heart a vow I had made to Him.

It was a hot summer day, not long after God had given me this acronym, *S.L.O.W.*

Kevin and I were on a little vacation, a couple of days away with some friends at their cabin. We had spent some much needed time at the beach and rode around the large lake on a pontoon boat. We enjoyed the sun and the company of our dear friends. We read while lounging in beach chairs on the dock. We even took our son Troy and his friend for the few days away. It was a relaxing time away. We had a great deal of fun.

On our way home we decided to stop and have fun with the boys. We wanted to play mini golf, ride some go-carts, and enjoy a few arcade games. The plan was to have fun. I'm not exactly sure what happened; things were going just fine, but somehow out of nowhere I turned into a crabby wife. The sweet, enjoyable, fun, smiling Ellen was replaced by a crabby woman. (I'm sure you have no idea what I'm referring to here. Perhaps you've never encountered this before. One moment all is fine and the next moment something overtakes your body and your mind, some awful personality switch occurs.) For the sake of this example let's just say you understand.

Anyway, Kevin's wife (that would be me) disappeared, and I was replaced by Mrs. Crab. I initiated some spat in the car on the way to the place o' fun, so when we pulled into the parking lot Kevin vacated the vehicle rather quickly and went with the boys into the arcade. I was left to trail behind, to fend for myself and that jacked up the crab-o-meter a few notches. I got out of the car, slammed the door and in my haste and nasty attitude realized I had left the camera in the car. (How taking pictures of this happy-moment-in-time was even on my radar is a mystery.) I did one of those Darth Vader breathing maneuvers; some would call it a heavy sigh. I walked back to the car and grabbed the camera slamming the poor car door, again, and turned to walk into the place o' fun all by myself. I didn't take very many steps, when I tripped.

God tripped me.

What?! He wouldn't do that. Well, I believe He did. I didn't get hurt. After all, there was no apparent reason that caused me to trip. There were no rocks or bumps of any kind in my path. But there was still a huge obstacle in my way. My attitude was in the way in this place o' fun. My attitude was my obstacle. God needed to get my attention. He had some rewriting to do on my heart. So He tripped me.

How do I know it was God Who did the tripping? Well, because as soon as I stumbled it was a natural reaction to look down and see what tripped me up. What did my eyes see? What was I gazing at? Short of using an airplane with a huge banner flying behind it, God used that very parking lot to rewrite on my heart. He reminded me of a vow I had made to Him. As I looked down this is what I saw right in front of me:

S.L.O.W. Livin'

In huge yellow letters painted on the cracked, once-black-now-gray asphalt was a message, a reminder from God. With the camera I had in my hand I took a picture. That picture has been used many times to bring me back to where God would have me. It's used as a screen saver on my computers. It's been turned into jewelry pendants. It's been given to ladies at speaking engagements and retreats. I use this word as my mantra, a repeated phrase I choose to live by. I turned this one word into a phrase and use it as my texting and email signature.

S.L.O.W. Livin'

Like the Hebrew midwives, Shiphrah and Puah, I desire to **SLOW**ly live out beauty and splendor. As I live **S.L.O.W.**, as I **fear**

God, I live in beauty and splendor. Preparation for the crisis comes by **S.L.O.W.** livin'.

I choose to fear God.

I choose to live **S.L.O.W.**

I choose to **S**erve God, **L**ove God,
Observe His commands, **W**alk in all His ways.

No matter what.
Even in times of crisis.

When my doctor told me we'd talk after Thanksgiving I was a bit surprised to see his office number on my caller ID the morning of November 20th, 6 days before Thanksgiving. My husband and I were hours away from spending a weekend with just the two of us. Our oldest daughter was a sophomore at Indiana Wesleyan University. She sang in a choir and they had a concert that weekend. Kevin and I designed our weekend away to coincide with her concert. We were leaving that Friday afternoon, right after a funeral Kevin was officiating. The bags were packed and the boys were taken care of for the weekend. We were ready for a few days away.

Four days away with just Kevin and myself. Ahhh.

But the caller ID disrupted that 'ahhh' feeling.

God never reveals His Word to His children without a purpose. God's Word comes from Him. He designed it. He initiates it. He speaks it. He made sure it was written down as one avenue to know Him. Isaiah 55:11 (NIV) says that "...His Word...will not return to Him empty, but will accomplish what He desires and achieves the purpose for which He sent it."

God sent His Word to Shiphrah & Puah. He revealed His Word to those two women. Likewise, God revealed His Word to me. He introduced these two gutsy women to me. He revealed their character to me and He did so with purpose. The lesson of how to not fall to pieces in a crisis wasn't just for knowledge sake alone. It wasn't to fill the what-I-know-so-I-can-win-a-Bible-trivia-test bucket. I didn't come to know Proverbs 24:10 on my own. I didn't find Deuteronomy 10:12-13 on my own. I wasn't introduced to Shiphrah and Puah just to find two gutsy women. Each of these discoveries was in reality a revelation.

Whenever we find a verse in Scripture that meets our current need, or we discover a new truth about any Bible character, or we turn a key thought into an acronym we must be careful to not take any credit for our creativity. God is the Revealer of His Word. As His revelation comes it is our responsibility to handle it correctly.

I had a responsibility as soon as I saw the caller ID. My responsibility? To decide if I would fall to pieces or fall on the preparation I had experienced prior to the crisis. I wasn't expecting a call from my doctor for two more weeks. That he was calling was cause for concern. So I tucked in tight to the truth of *S.L.O.W.* I tucked tight into the role-modeling of two Hebrew midwives and I tucked the revealed Word of God tight into my heart and I answered the phone.

CHAPTER 3

Pondering the Crisis

"Hello?" I answered.

"Ellen, this is Julie, from Dr. H's office. He would like to talk to you today. Could you come into the office this morning?"

"Sure, what time would you like me there?"

"What time is convenient for you?"

Wait. Did my doctor's nurse just ask what time would work for me? I never had that happen before. In all my experiences of calling doctor offices I have never been asked what time would work best.

"I can be there in 40 minutes." She said they would see me then.

I called Kevin. "Hey Babe, Dr. H just called and wants to chat with me."

"Ok, I'll see what I can do about the funeral."

My husband is a good man.

"Babe, that's not necessary. What could he possibly have to tell me that I can't tell you when I see you later today? You keep your plans for the day and we'll connect later, besides, he probably just wants to take my uterus out and frankly, that's ok, I don't need it anymore." (Insert chuckles from both of us. Remember we're still on the adoption plan. My uterus wasn't necessary for acquiring more children through adoption.)

Off to the doctor I go.
And the pondering begins.

Just what does it mean to *ponder*?

Definition #1 (from dictionary.com): "to consider something deeply and thoroughly."

I was deeply considering what I would hear when I saw the doctor. Pondering is not for "what will I wear today" or "what flavor latte should I order" or "what should I pull out of the freezer for dinner." Those are considerations, simple daily choices.

Pondering is for deep, thorough, careful thought.

In the Bible, 'ponder' is used a few times, mostly in the Old Testament, though it is used once in the New Testament. In Luke 2:19 (NIV) we find this verb. "Mary treasured up all these things and *pondered* them in her heart."

Mary is a young lady, a teen-aged girl really. She had just given birth to the Son of God, in a stable, after a long journey on foot, and riding on the back of a donkey. Nine months prior she had received a visit from an angel of God. The angel, being God's messenger, had told Mary she was chosen by God to be the virgin that would give birth to His Son. God had chosen her to be the mother of His Son. God had chosen her to be the one to carry the Savior of the world in her womb and then deliver Him into the world. What followed that message was months of activity and preparation.

And now she's in a stable, her baby is wrapped in swaddling cloths and lying in a manger. A bright star is shining in the sky. Shepherds have just visited and are now spreading the news, proclaiming glory and praise for what they had been told and had now witnessed. Mary is a new mommy. What an angel had told her months prior has occurred - exactly how the angel had said it would happen.

And Mary *ponders*.

Mary chooses to deeply and thoroughly consider what has happened. Nine months ago she was giddy, newly in love with a young man named Joseph, and they were most likely contemplating marriage. One day in her seemingly ordinary life, an angel shows up; *an angel, of Holy God*, shows up with a message from Holy God. A message that to most would seem ridiculous, impossible; a message that would make most young girls run for their lives attempting to get far away from God's angel and His message.

God chose Mary because she was highly favored. God delighted and found pleasure in the way she lived her life. And she was willing to be used of God to bring the Savior of the world into the world through her. She was willing to be obedient, to become pregnant, not through the natural way, but by the Power of God, through the Holy Spirit. Mary responded to God saying to the angel, "I am the Lord's servant, may it be to me as you have said." Luke 1:38 (NIV)

And it was.

She is now a mother; a mommy, not to just any child; to God's Son. She has just given birth to Emmanuel, God with us! God now has skin on and He's her responsibility to take care of. She will take care of this Babe. She will raise Him, teach Him, guide Him, and meet His physical needs. She will raise the Son of God, Jesus, Savior of the World. God chose her for this assignment. He chose her for this God-sized task.

Mary could have chosen to panic. Mary could have chosen to question. Mary could have chosen to reconsider. But Mary made her choice. At first she was frightened by the angel's appearance. But it didn't take long for her troubled heart to be calmed by the angel's presence and words. And she responded to the angel's message that she had been chosen, by God, to be the mother of Jesus. She willingly said yes to God.

And now she ponders.

Mary pondered because her task, her assignment, required careful, deep, thorough consideration of what would happen next. Mary is a role model to us.

Mary models for us how to respond. Mary teaches us that when God has a task that comes with great difficulty and may even seem impossible that we too should ponder. We should give careful, deep, thorough consideration to the task that looms or to the crisis that presents itself. Know ahead of time how you'll want to respond to a crisis.

That doesn't mean emotionless. The suggestion isn't you can't shed tears or be angry. It doesn't mean pull-up-your-big-girl-panties-and-deal-with-it. Pondering helps in not falling to pieces when a crisis comes. Pondering is crucial. Pondering allows for consideration of appropriate and godly action to a situation, to a crisis; instead of a reaction.

On my way to the doctor I listened to Christian radio. I wasn't even a mile into the 20 mile drive when a familiar song came on the radio. A song my dear friend, Jenny, had recently introduced me to. Jenny & I were worship/song leaders at a weekend women's event a month before this particular day in November. As it often happens, we sang many songs over the course of that weekend but there was one that stood alone, one song that resonated with each person in attendance. God's Spirit used this particular song to minister His peace, His mercy, and His faithfulness into each soul. It was this same song that *just happened* to be playing on the radio as I was in my vehicle that day; Chris Tomlin's "I Will Rise."

Ponder. Oh, did I ponder.

One phrase in the song says, "There's a peace I've come to know..."

And I pondered some more.

Another phrase says, "There's an anchor for my soul..."

More pondering.

And then, "...I can say, 'it is well'..."

My heart latched on to that phrase. *It is well.*

As a woman who was headed to a spontaneous meeting with her doctor, who had no idea what she was about to hear, God was speaking into my heart. He was preparing me and I wasn't really aware of it.

Hindsight writes these words and I experience that moment all over again. As you're quite aware hindsight is 20/20. It is perfect vision. I now have perfect vision of that moment. However, at the time my vision was quite skewed. I had no clue what was coming in less than an hour. God knew. God allowed a song to be played with a message He knew I needed.

He spoke His Word into me through a song and I was able to ponder. I can't tell you that my exact thoughts were "If I fall to pieces in a crisis there wasn't much to me in the first place," because I'd be lying. I wasn't thinking that at all. Thinking involves planning. Thinking requires action.

I was pondering. Pondering considers; deeply considers. Pondering settled me. I settled my soul on His *peace.* I was *anchored* in the knowledge that *it is well.*

No matter what.

I arrive at the doctor's office and I'm the only one in the waiting room. There's one receptionist, Julie the nurse, and Dr. H. Later I found out that Dr. H asked that they meet at this particular office just for me, seeing as it's normally closed on a Friday. They opened this office for me, for this appointment, so I wouldn't have to travel the extra 15 miles to the main office.

I love my doctor. Especially considering, I was a new patient. When I went to him in mid-October it was the first time I had met him. When he ordered the ultrasound and then the hysteroscopy, he did it because "his gut told him to." (I know Who was speaking to his gut and it wasn't a medical journal.)

"Ellen, you can come back with me," Julie says. She led me to a room and said, "Have a seat and Doc will be right with you."

I didn't wait long at all seeing as I was the only patient in the whole office.

Dr. H enters the room, holding a manila folder/chart, takes a seat on the roll-y chair, rolls over to where I'm sitting, shakes my hand with a friendly "Hello, Ellen," and looks me in the eye. "I can't believe I'm about to tell you this, but Ellen, you have cancer."

There it was.

Cancer? Bam! Like a punch in the gut the news was delivered.
Crisis? Cancer.
Crisis.

There's a peace I've come to know.

I immediately took out a piece of paper and a pen from my purse and began writing things down. There was a great deal of information.

- Stage 2 endometrial (uterine) cancer; with spread to the cervix

There's an anchor for my soul.

- a gynecologic oncologist is needed and referred (a doctor who treats women with cancer affecting their reproductive organs)
- clear cell carcinoma (at the time I had no clue what that meant, but later found it to mean I had a rare form of uterine cancer that is aggressive and has a high recurrence rate)
- high risk and aggressive
- complete hysterectomy necessary
- chemotherapy
- radiation

I can say, "it is well."

With loads of information, notes scratched on a piece of paper in my purse, and hugs from Julie and Dr. H, I was back in my vehicle.

I sat in my mini-van and cried some not-so-mini tears. I cried hard. I fell to pieces? No. I cried. Tears fell, and that's all that fell. I cried and God heard.

There's a peace I've come to know.

It took some time but I was ready for the journey back home. instead of turning the radio on I called Kevin. Even as I write this I'm crying. Not tears of sadness. Not tears of bad memories. Rather, tears of wow-I-have-an-amazing-husband. Tears of remembering the emotions of *how will we tell the kids*. Tears of *whoa, how do you tell your parents something like this*? Tears of *never saw that coming*. Tears of confusion since we thought we had heard God's call to adopt but would now need to close our case file.

Tears fell. But that didn't mean I fell to pieces.

"Kevin, honey, I have…it's not good…I have cancer." And I cried. Kevin's response? "Oh, Babe, get home so I can hold you and we can talk. I love you so much. I vowed I would be devoted to you through sickness and in health. Nothing changes that. I am, and always will be, devoted to you."

Pondering the crisis.
Ponder.

Definition #2: to weigh carefully in the mind; consider thoughtfully.

Now that the crisis was before me, now that the crisis had arrived, I pondered once again. Only that time I was no longer pondering the unknown, I was *weighing carefully* what had become my reality, my crisis. An hour earlier I had uttered the *words* "What could he possibly have to tell me that I can't tell you when I see you later today?" Now I know what *he could possibly have to tell me*. My response?

In my journal I wrote this: *Since October 29 when I began bleeding, I have had a peace to the very bottom of my soul...oh, there's uncertainty, questions, scared moments; but the foundation of my soul is peace.*

I weighed carefully in my mind many things. I considered many things.

When studying the Bible I like to know what a particular word means in the original language it was written in. It allows me a greater understanding of the meaning and message. The New Testament of the Bible was originally written in Greek. When I look up the verb *ponder* in Greek I find the word *sumballo*, which literally means *to bring together in one's mind, to confer with one's self.*

Now I feel better about all those times I find I'm having a conversation with me. Is it that I'm really just *sumballo*? Our English word *ponder* is to weigh carefully in the mind. The Greek equivalent takes it a step further, it implies to actually have a conversation with oneself about what is on one's mind. That's exactly what I did after Kevin and I hung up, I conferred with me. The definition of *confer* is *to consult together; compare opinions; carry on a discussion.*

Conferring resulted in me deciding that I would not fall to pieces in this crisis. From that day forward, I decided that my crisis would be used to lead others to the Christ.

No matter what.

A week after the surgery which consisted of a total hysterectomy along with lymph node and pelvic washing removal (for pathology inspection), Kevin and I were headed back to the gynecologic oncologist for the post-surgery pathology report. That means the doctor will tell us what the exact diagnosis, prognosis and treatment will be. Early that morning I was reading my Bible. It was December 16th, so I was reading Psalm 16.

Since God's Word is revealed to us, I just love when the Revealer reveals His truth, His Word, to me. I love reading His Word. I love when I learn new things from His Word. That happens often, learning new things while reading my Bible. Having God's Words revealed to me; having them applied to my life by His Spirit, at just the right moment, for just the right circumstance, exactly when and where I need His Words; they never disappoint, they're never late, they're never absent. On this particular morning, December 16, 2009, I had a revelation, a unique experience of His Word attaching to my life, to my heart, like I've never had before.

I was reading early in the morning. I was alone in the living room, curled up in a recliner. I was the only one awake, therefore, it was quiet. I opened my Bible, turned to Psalm 16 and began reading. After I read verse five, I stopped. I actually couldn't read any further. My eyes were glued to verse five, they were stuck staring at one word in that verse.

This one word seemed to stand out from all the rest. It was as if the word were raised up higher than all the other words in front of me. It kind of jumped off the page. Never before had a passage from God's Word seemingly jumped off the page and attached to my heart.

It was as if this one word turned into a bold script, right before my eyes, and popped up off the page of my Bible. I physically responded to what I had just read. I startled, not out of fear or surprise, rather, out of awe that God had just revealed His Word to me. I responded to that one word. Just one word, in Psalm 16:5. I reacted to how this word popped off the page and slammed into me. All of my senses were on high alert. It was like my eyes only focused on it, my mouth ate it up, my nose inhaled it, my ears heard it, and my body enveloped by it. That word?

Assigned

Psalm 16:5 (NIV) "Lord, You have **assigned** me my portion and my cup, You have made my lot secure."

There it was. *Assigned*. Like a calm gentle breeze, God's voice followed the abrupt word-jumping/popping experience that had just occurred. His voice settled in my soul. He gave me something else to ponder, something else to weigh carefully, to consider thoughtfully.

Cancer was His *assignment* for me.
This crisis was my assignment.

And He allowed it. He allowed it so that His Son, my Savior, Jesus Christ, could be glorified. He allowed it so that others might be led to the Christ through my crisis.

I still ponder this. If I try to see this through my eyes, my understanding, it doesn't make sense and then I'm susceptible to falling to pieces in the crisis. Pondering is weighing carefully. Pondering is considering thoughtfully. I still weigh it. I still consider it.

God assigned cancer to me. He didn't cause it. He didn't give it. He *assigned* it, for His purpose. He *assigned* it, for His Son to be glorified through it. He **assigned** it, so that **others could be led to the Christ through my crisis.** My portion and my cup were **assigned** to me, from Holy God, and He used His Word to reveal this truth to me.

When I sat in Dr. H's office and heard for the first time "you have cancer" God was not sitting on His throne in heaven, shocked, startled, or even freaked out. He didn't exclaim, "Oh no! Now what are we gonna do?" Before the surgeon removed the cancer, before the pathologist looked at the cells under a microscope, God held my assignment.

God filtered this crisis through His fingers and allowed the cancer to be my crisis. It wasn't random. It wasn't a sick joke. I hadn't committed some sin that caused me to earn such a punishment. Something happened inside my body, a high risk, aggressive cancer attached to my uterus, and it grew and it spread. God knew it. God allowed it. God assigned it. This crisis, called cancer, was my assignment.

Did she just say God assigned her a crisis? Why, yes she did. Yes, I did. And I pondered that thought, I weighed that thought, I carefully considered that thought. I still ponder that thought. Providence, a foreseeing guidance and care, provided a way for me to trust in my Lord in a way I had never experienced before. Providence provided a way for me to not only teach about how to not fall to pieces in a crisis, but to also live out what God had revealed to me prior to the crisis showing up. I still ponder this thought.

You see, though I had cancer, it never had me. My Lord had me. He held me. My Lord still has me, all of me, and He still holds me. God's Word is clear that His children are held in the palm of His hand. Isaiah 49:16 (NIV) says, "We're engraved on the palms of His hands." The word *engrave* in this verse means to inscribe, to set, or to mark. That should make us giddy. That should cause excitement to bubble up and spill out of our lives. That should make us want to stand up and cheer, fist-pump, and high-five Holy God!

God's children are engraved on His hand. His children are set on the very palm that placed the stars in the sky. We are marked on the very hand that tells the ocean when to stop at the shore. We are tattooed on the hand that hung the moon and carved the mountain ranges. These thoughts, these ponderings, excite me.

Isaiah 40 describes how the very hand you're engraved on is the same hand that can mark off the heavens with a hand-breadth. That would be like a basketball player palming a basketball; picking up and holding a basketball by spreading his very large hand across the ball and gripping it with his thumb on one side and his pinky finger on the other. God does that with the earth. He's got the whole world in His Hand? Isaiah says He does. WOW!

Isaiah also describes that you are inscribed on the very palm of the same hand that can measure the waters of the whole earth in the hollow of His hand. As humans we're capable of holding maybe a few tablespoons of water in the palm of our hand. God is capable, according to Isaiah 40:12, of measuring the waters, measuring *the* waters. That word picture is really too big for our imaginations. We can cup maybe 3 - 4 tablespoons of water in our palm. He can cup over 332.5 million cubic miles of water in His palm. What's a cubic mile? Does it really matter? It's a lot!! It's more than 4 tablespoons. However, one cubic mile of water equals more than 1.1 trillion gallons. Amazing!

I read somewhere that if all the water on earth (oceans, icecaps and glaciers, lakes, rivers, groundwater, and water in the atmosphere) were made into a ball of water, the diameter of that ball would be about 860 miles long. That's a big ball. An 860 mile diameter - a straight line passing through the center of that water ball would be the distance from Chicago to somewhere in Virginia, or say Miami to somewhere in Tennessee, or Detroit to Sioux Falls, SD. That's a really long, straight line.

And our God, the One who can hold that water ball, the one with an 860 mile diameter in the palm of His hand, is the same God who held my cancer in His hands. He held it and then it filtered through His fingers and fell on me. He assigned it to me.

Nothing happens in one of God's children's lives without Holy God's permission and knowledge. He was well aware of my crisis. He assigned it to me. He assigned, and He allowed, the crisis. He didn't give me cancer. He assigned a crisis, in hope that others would be led to the Christ through my crisis.

Is God able to take care of His children? Does He know best? Is it possible for a crisis to be an assignment from Holy God? Is it possible to have a complete and utter trust in the Lord *no matter what*? Is He able to hold you in the palm of His hand instead of you falling to pieces in a crisis? When a crisis comes does He have all things in His vision, under His watchful, and tender care? Is He able to handle all the details, whether little or big, that are left in the wake of a crisis?

Things to ponder.

Prior to this crisis Kevin and I were on the road to adoption. We just *knew* that was the assignment for our family. We *knew* God had called us to it. How did we get that wrong? Yet, I was so sure that this new assignment was straight from the omniscient, all-knowing, God.

Pondering caused us to realize we needed to call Pam, our adoption case worker, and have our case file closed. That broke our hearts. It was a difficult phone call to make, but a detail God had on His radar. We were confused, but He was in charge.

Not only did we know we couldn't bring new children into such a confusing crisis but the agency and our state has a policy that adoptive parents need to be healthy to allow for a stable environment for children coming out of tragic situations, crises of their own.

The timing, the diagnosis, the crisis didn't make sense. But it still made sense to trust in the One Who is the same yesterday, today and forever; trusting in the One Who held us tight in the palm of His hand; trusting in the One Who many people over many years have trusted in because He is able, He is stable, and He is faithful.

Ponder that!

CHAPTER 4

People Surrounding the Crisis

I love personality profiles. I love seeing what makes people tick. I love to know why people act, react, or respond to situations based on how they're wired. During my crisis I loved seeing how God surrounded me with people as one of His ways to saturate me with His love.

I love watching people use their talents for His purposes. There are scores of people who meet basic, everyday needs in a crisis and to a person in the crisis these people are heroes. The meals, the favors, those who did laundry, those who sent cards, those who helped clean house, the social media comments and encouragements, those who taxied my kids around, the flowers, those who sat with me while having chemo, those who visited...oh my, the list goes on.

Throughout my crisis I was blessed beyond measure. Blessing after blessing came; all through people being Jesus-with-skin-on to me. I saw His reflection in every act of kindness that was directed to me.

I would love to list each blessing brought my way through so many different people but I feel as if I'd be like the actress attempting to thank each person right after she won the coveted award. She mentally runs through the list of all those she'd like to thank but inevitably someone gets missed, innocently left out.

If I attempted to list each blessing I know I'd miss someone, but even more, there simply isn't enough room in this book to list each one. The cards themselves total in the hundreds. Some are from repeat senders, but still, hundreds of blessings through cards. I still have each one, saved in a special place, conveniently located, so I can read them whenever the need arises.

Years before I had cancer I was in one of my favorite stores. This particular store begins with a T and ends in a Maxx. I love to shop their clearance racks, especially in the house goods section. I found this really funky looking box-like object that resembles a briefcase. Its purpose in my home was to sit and look good while taking up space. It really didn't have a significant purpose. I bought it because it had a red sticker on it and was marked down to $7.00 from $35.00. Something that inexpensive and that funky needed a home. It needed to be in my home, even if it didn't have a recognized purpose at the moment.

As soon as the cards started coming in, this once purposeless case now had a purpose. To this day it sits in my living room filled with love, filled with blessings. If you aren't careful, as it's opened, cards will spill out. These cards represent love that goes beyond our human capabilities, a love that comes only from God. It's a specific kind of love.

It's called Agape. *Pronunciation: uh-GAH-pay.*

Agape is exemplified by the kind of love Jesus Christ has for His Father and for His followers. It's selfless, sacrificial and unconditional. And this love surrounded me in my crisis. But agape cannot show up without a source. Agape requires people. Agape comes from God but is displayed through people. Agape held and hugged me.

1Corinthians, chapter 13, is often referred to as the love chapter in Scripture. The word *love* in the Bible is translated with different meanings. In chapter 13 of 1Corinthians the word is translated to agape. This chapter is written in a letter from a guy named Paul to a church in a place called Corinth. Paul is encouraging and teaching the people, church people in Corinth, how to love like Jesus loves.

Within this chapter I read love is kind, love is not self-seeking, love protects, love never fails. The same love described here is what I experienced first hand in my crisis. People were kind. People met our needs. People protected. People never gave up on me. People loved. People showed agape love. People surrounded me in my crisis.

Calling Pam was difficult. I still remember making that call. It was heart wrenching. Even now as I am writing this, I can still feel the heaviness of that moment. I remember hanging up the phone and praying for my kids, the ones I hadn't met yet. Kevin and I were still confused. We just knew adoption was THE option for us. But here I was crying because I had just told Pam I had cancer and our file needed to be closed. Ugh. What about the kids God had chosen us to be parents for? What about those kids that needed a forever family?

When a crisis comes, is not the time to focus on the future. What do I mean by that? Making big decisions or setting major goals are not things that should be focused on. Rather, living in the moment, one day at a time, is the best idea.

Kevin and I needed to simply push the adoption option to the back of our minds. We didn't forget it, we didn't give up on it, we didn't really even talk about it; we just set it aside and left it there. God protected us in this area. He somehow, in His great mercy, closed people's mouths. As we were surrounded by people in our crisis we were never burdened with questions of "what now?" in regards to adopting. That was another significant way people surrounded us with agape love.

The day I sat in Dr. H's office and heard those three life-altering words, you have cancer, was a day that even now seems like it went in slow motion. From the moment I entered that office I was surrounded by people in my crisis. I was surrounded by Dr. H and Julie as they reported the diagnosis.

I was also surrounded by my sweet man, my husband, as he told me to hurry up and get home so he could hold me. And he did. I walked in the house and fell in his arms. My husband's arms are the safest place on earth for me. We held each other as we cried. Then he prayed.

Not one time through this crisis did I ever hear my husband doubt, never did he ask why, and never did he show anger toward God. My husband never fell to pieces in our crisis. I did not just say that everything was wonderful. It wasn't. We cried, we hurt, we fought, we argued, we were frustrated at times. However, crying, hurting, fighting, arguing, frustration does not equal falling to pieces.

When I am asked what I love or appreciate about my husband my very first response is always the same. Without missing a beat I say, "His integrity." Kevin is the real deal. I love this quality about him, especially as a husband, a dad, and as a pastor. I love that the same man in the pulpit is the same man in our living room, the same man in the bleachers at a sporting event is the same man while in a counseling session, the same man officiating at a wedding or a funeral is the same man at a community function, and the same man at the gym is the same man our kids call daddy.

I was surrounded by this integrity as Kevin held me at the beginning of my crisis. As we stood crying, praying, and holding each other I knew Kevin and I were determined not to fall to pieces in this crisis.

One of the ways I was surrounded by people in my crisis showed up as a blanket, a big, beautiful fleece blanket. It is lime green on one side and bright vibrant bold colors in a fun geometric pattern on the other side. It's one of those blankets that have many sets of tied tassels surrounding the entire blanket.

This blanket was presented to me one Sunday morning after church. It was a couple of weeks after my surgery and prior to my first chemo treatment. I had just gone to the front of the sanctuary to gather my things and as I turned around to leave a dear sister in Christ was walking towards me. I must insert here what was on my mind at this precise moment as I was gathering my things.

You see, prior to this crisis I didn't cry very easily. Oh, I shed tears at sappy chick flicks. I even shed tears at weddings as I watch the groom watch his bride coming down the aisle. (We actually attempt to sit where we can get the best glimpse of the groom for this very purpose.) I cried when Kevin and I argued. Other than that, crying didn't come easily.

Until the crisis. Until I was surrounded by people, presenting me with God's agape love. Then it didn't take much for the tears to flow. I love this new change since my crisis. I wasn't broken or insensitive before, but somehow God knew what I needed and He provided it at the right times. I used to not cry very easily. That was ok. Now I cry. And it's ok.

As I turned around in the sanctuary and saw this special lady carrying a blanket and walking towards me, I began to cry. Gentle tears came. They escaped out of my eyes and ran down my cheeks. She said, "Ellen, I made this blanket for you right after your diagnosis was announced. It's been in the church office for weeks. Each one of these tassels has been tied by someone different in the church. As they tied the tassel they prayed for you." Yup. More tears.

I treasure this blanket. I love this blanket. That blanket with those tassels surrounded me as I sat hooked up to a machine that injected chemicals into my body. Like the people who surrounded that blanket with agape love toward me tying a tassel and praying for me, that blanket surrounded me at different times during my crisis.

surrounded by agape love

I was diagnosed on a Friday. I came home to be held by Kevin, yet our three boys were home that day as well. Our daughter, Christine, was away at college. When Kevin and I had finished praying we gathered the boys in our living room and shared our news with them.

Here is one of the biggest reasons why I am so grateful the Lord impressed upon me that falling to pieces in a crisis proves there isn't much to you in the first place: I had an audience. My four kids were watching their mom deal with a crisis. They were paying attention to how I handled this crisis. And I wasn't about to fall to pieces. I wanted my crisis to help lead my kids closer to the Christ. They became my barometer, my measurer of pressure.

Our oldest son, the second born, is Andrew. At the time of my crisis he was an 18 year old, recent high school graduate, who was attending a community college and hating it. He was struggling with where he should be and what he should be doing in life. Determining goals, visions, and motivations were difficult for him at that time. Then this crisis hits. It wasn't easy watching him struggle. There were some tense moments in our home.

One day Andrew and I collided. Not physically, but emotionally and verbally. Two passionately, strong-willed, hurting people collided. That rarely ends well. The result of that confrontation was me running to my bedroom, collapsing on my bed, and having an emotional breakdown. I fell to pieces? NO! I was mad, frustrated and hurt; therefore, I cried. That's not falling to pieces.

I was lying on my bed and my sweet husband gently entered the room. He was carrying *the blanket*. Kevin lay down next to me, covered us both in the beautiful blanket, picked up a tassel, placed it in my hand, wrapped his bigger, stronger hand over mine and quietly said, "I wonder if this is the tassel Andrew held while he prayed for his momma."

Whew. I can't even put into words what happened at that moment. What I know is a woman, a mom, with cancer, who had recently gone through surgery and complications connected to it, a woman surrounded by all kinds of unknowns, a lady in the middle of a crisis was suddenly surrounded by God's agape love in the form of a big, beautiful blanket. In our family we apologize, we love, we respect each other, and we extend grace.

Where is my son, Andrew now? At the writing of this book, Andrew is actively serving his country as a United States Marine. I couldn't be more proud of him.

Telling our kids their mom had cancer was not an easy task. It wasn't easy watching them cry, it wasn't easy watching them struggle with such difficult news. My boys immediately surrounded me with hugs, love, and words of encouragement. We banded together. We determined without words, only actions, that this wasn't going to be our undoing, it would be something we would allow to draw us closer together. We were going to walk this journey together.

Right after we told the boys I called Christine. I didn't like sharing this kind of news over the phone but we wanted her to be on the same page as us and on the same time line, as well. We were anxious to see her the following day. We so wanted to be surrounded by each other. Surrounded, gathered, and banded together as a family.

Our weekend away with just Kevin and I turned into a weekend away as a family. Though it may seem trivial to some, we saw God's protective hand on our family that weekend. He knew ahead of time that we didn't need to be at our home church, that Kevin didn't need to be preaching, and He provided a weekend away for us to just simply be together.

We worshiped together at a church in another state, where we knew no one. What a blessing to be able to sit next to my preacher husband as we worshiped on the Sunday right after a crisis entered our lives. While we sang, we held hands and cried. The words in the songs, the words of the preacher, and sitting as a family was a balm to our hurting hearts. We were surrounded and soothed by each other's presence in the pew that Sunday.

On December 16th we were on our way to the post-surgery, pathology report appointment. While backing out of the driveway Kevin decided to get the mail before we left. I was annoyed. Couldn't the mail wait? We were on our way to a very important appointment. I was on edge because I was focused on the upcoming appointment and still in pain from the surgery. It was a recipe for being on edge but it wasn't an excuse for being annoyed with my husband. You see, in my annoyance and in my edginess, I could have very well missed a blessing, a gift straight from God.

Kevin didn't just walk to the mailbox in his regular fashion of retrieving the mail. As we backed out of the driveway he pulled up to the mailbox like it was a pick-up window at a fast food restaurant. I'm so glad he did. I was still in the pondering mode from receiving God's revelation to me that I was on assignment from Him. And that quickly changed to the annoyance mode from Kevin feeling pulled in the direction of the mailbox.

He pulled up to the mailbox, took out what was inside, and placed a package on my lap. It was like he had pulled up to the speaker of the fast food place and said, "I'd like a blessing for my wife and could you please super size that?"

As I looked down at the package I didn't recognize the return address. After opening the over-stuffed, thick envelope sitting on my lap was what looked like a handmade skinny afghan. It had been crocheted or knitted (don't judge me, but I have no clue which is which). After I read the enclosed card I knew exactly what it was. A prayer shawl. From strangers. A super-sized blessing from God.

People I had never met gifted me. Faces I had never seen, from a church miles away, chose the yarn, took the time to create this gorgeous piece of comfort, pray over it, and sent it to me. And I almost missed a blessing from these sweet strangers who surrounded me in my crisis.

I'm an extrovert. At the beginning of this chapter I mentioned I liked personality profiles that show how people are wired. On every profile I've ever taken I score high, really high, on the area of extroversion. I have a friend whose husband affectionately calls me, and her, "an introvert's nightmare." I think he's crazy. That's not the point.

Being an extrovert means that I intentionally surround myself with people. I have friends, lots of them. That's not a bragging comment. It's a reality for an extrovert. Friends play different roles in our lives. It's like an archery target. Lots of arrows fit on the target and as you get closer to the center only a few are able to fit.

Friends are the same way. A lot of friends fit in our lives but only a few can settle in the very center. In girl circles we refer to these as best friends. Girls in the very center of your bull's eye are those ladies who cause you to be a better person and likewise. The girls in the center of my bull's eye challenge me in my relationship with Christ. They are the ones I can count on to push me closer to Him, they encourage me to become more like Him, they are my cheerleaders, they are my confidants, they make me laugh, they comfort me when I cry, they tell me the truth, they give me Godly, Biblical wisdom, and they were attentive in my crisis. They surrounded me with the kind of love only best friends can shower on each other. I needed them and they showed up; at just the right time.

Again, I would need more room to name all the friends who touched my life, who surrounded me in particular ways during my crisis. I simply cannot name them all, but I will highlight a couple of ladies who illustrate what surrounding a friend in her crisis looks like.

They showed up at just the right time. They were assigned to me at exactly the moment I needed them on my assignment. They are a huge part of the reason why I didn't fall to pieces in my crisis. Proverbs 24:10 says, we fall to pieces because there wasn't much to us in the first place. Surrounding yourself with the right people, allowing the right people in the center of your bull's eye is critical when faced with a crisis.

Jenny is one of the ladies who surrounded me in this crisis. She's a friend that is permanently smack dab in the middle of my bull's eye of friends. I love how God smashed our lives together. We met while my husband was serving as pastor at the church her family was attending years earlier. Our friendship had just begun to blossom and grow roots when Kevin was appointed to a different community to serve as pastor. We ignored the geographical space and continued to work on our growing friendship.

Jenny makes me a better person. Jenny makes me want to be a better person. Jenny and I connect on so many different levels. We each strive to love our husbands in ways that please God. We love being moms, desiring to be godly examples to our children. We're committed to our friendship and we take time to pour into each other's lives. We love being in ministry together, her leading music and me speaking and teaching. We can share anything with each other. We really love to be silly together. We can make each other laugh when it makes zero sense to others around us. She's the first person I call when I have a celebration. And she was the first person, after my family, to hear of my crisis. She's the same Jenny who taught me the song that ministered to me on my way to the doctor.

Though she lived over an hour away she was at my doorstep the very day I was diagnosed. I remember her walking into my house and us hugging. Her presence was consistent throughout my crisis. She sent cards, many of them. Most made me laugh. All had a hand-written note of encouragement and love that could only come from a center-of-the-bull's-eye-kind of friend.

I love to notice how God works in the small things. It's easy to stand at the foot of a mountain or at the shore of the ocean or in a sunrise/sunset and notice God's handiwork on display. I like to focus on one blade of grass out of the whole yard. I like to stare at one star in the entire sky. I like to concentrate on one snowflake at a time that will settle with millions of others to form a gorgeous blanket of white on the ground. I see God's handiwork in the simple, yet so complex to understand things. When I step back and take a peek at God's hand in my crisis I like to notice Him in the simple things. Recognizing Him in the apparent small things actually makes Him seem that much bigger.

One of the apparent simple and small ways God showed up in my crisis was where my doctor, the oncologist was geographically located and therefore, where I had my chemo treatments. Jenny, my center-of-the-bull's-eye-who-lived-many-miles-away friend, worked minutes from the treatment center. My chemo treatments were hours long, but Jenny took her lunch break each time to sit with me, bringing food and gifts, like matching lime green purses. Just because. Being able to spend those difficult moments with her made for a very precious gift to me. A small *surrounding of people*, and yet a huge treasure at a burdensome time in my crisis.

One of the best things Jenny has ever done for me was to encourage me to read God's Word after I was diagnosed. She suggested we read through the Psalms together, beginning with Psalm 1 on December 1. So when I read Psalm 16 on December 16th and God revealed that this crisis was my assignment from him, it was because Jenny was faithful to encourage me to read the Psalms with her that month.

Jenny never treated me with caution, she knew how to sense each moment and each mood determining what was appropriate and necessary for the moment. Did the moment need laughter, silliness, quiet, chatting? She had the right radar for whatever the particular moment called for.

Our friendship didn't experience any speed bump in my crisis. Jenny carried my crisis with me; she wore my pain and shared my frustrations. She is the iron I need to sharpen my iron, Proverbs 27:17. Our friendship went even deeper as a result of her surrounding me in my crisis. "A friend loves at all times," Proverbs 17:17 says. That is exactly how Jenny surrounded me; with love, agape love, in my crisis.

my center of the bull's eye, Jenny

As an introvert's nightmare, an extreme extrovert, I love being surrounded by people in life. I loved being surrounded by people in my crisis. Some folks shy away from people, even the people they love, when a crisis comes. God designed us to need each other. He designed us to be interdependent. That means there are times when independence is called for and there are times when being dependent on others is acceptable, appropriate, and absolutely necessary.

The desire to tell as many friends as I could, as quickly as I could, was embedded deep within me. My crisis showed up on a Friday and by Sunday hundreds of people were praying for me, surrounding me with agape love.

Years ago there was a popular commercial for a hair product. The ad encouraged people to tell one to two friends about that particular shampoo. Then those friends would tell one to two other friends. And so on, and so on. The commercial would put faces in squares and as the camera panned out the number of squares increased, therefore more faces/people were finding out about this product. All because one friend told two friends.

That's how I felt with my crisis. I didn't want people to know so they could feel sorry for me. I didn't desire for people to hear so they could pity me and simply let others know, "Hey, did you hear about poor Ellen and her cancer?" NO! I wanted people to know so they could pray. I wanted people to hear so that my family could be surrounded by God's agape love.

I began calling my friends. I called those in the center of my bull's eye first. I knew that the level of support and love would go deep and spread far from these special ladies, these friends of mine. And they didn't fail, they didn't disappoint.

My only expectation from them was to share in my crisis, to help carry my load. Each lady that takes up space in the center of my bull's eye met that expectation. Each one uniquely and individually loved me, shared my burden, and surrounded me in my crisis.

CHAPTER 5

Persistence Through the Crisis

It's quite possible that I am strong willed woman. Ok, it's an absolute affirmative that I am a strong willed woman. It's a trait my parents often lost sleep over. It's a way of life my husband has a love/hate relationship with. (You should pray for him.) It's probably what keeps me sane as a mom of 6. It's what keeps me on the phone with customer service representatives for long periods of time getting what I feel is fair and right for less than acceptable service or treatment. And it's what definitely showed up in my crisis.

To those of you reading this book and are not strong willed; it's ok. God wired you the way He wired you and He will provide you with what you need in order to be persistent when it's necessary. I am grateful for the way God made me. One of the qualities God naturally instilled in me is persistence. My strong will, my persistence has been a close friend to me, especially through this crisis!

What exactly does it mean to be strong-willed?

It means **stubborn, resolute, obstinate.**

Now wait," some of you are silently saying, "And that's exactly why I'm glad I'm not strong willed." However, those of you who are strong willed are saying, "Yup, that's about it, and I'm proud of it, wouldn't have it any other way!"

Stubborn: *resolute; obstinately maintained*
Resolute: *set in purpose, determined*
Obstinate: *firmly or stubbornly adhering to one's purpose, characterized by inflexible persistence*

I find it interesting that two of the words contain one of the other words in its own definition. Stubborn has resolute as a defining word and obstinate has stubborn in its definition.

To capture the point of this chapter I combined and shortened these three definitions into one phrase to describe what I see as a strong-willed personality:

One who is firmly and stubbornly determined to maintain a purpose through persistence.

And there we find our focus for this chapter: persistence.

As I condense the definition even more here's what I have:

Persistence: *continuing steadfastly in some purpose.*

My goal was to not fall to pieces in my crisis. My purpose was so others could be pointed to the Christ through my crisis. By definition, that required continuing on steadfastly with that goal and that purpose as my gauge and my guide.

Persistence. Though I'm naturally wired to be persistent, with a strong will, I still need women as role models for me to discover how to do it the right way.

Jochebed is one of these women. She is a persistent woman. She is also another Woman Warrior from the Bible who has taught me more about doing the right thing, no matter what. She, too, has shown me how to not fall to pieces in a crisis. You may not know her name but perhaps you've heard of her son Moses.

The definition of persistence can be attached to this momma. She is one who firmly and stubbornly was determined to maintain a purpose by persistence: in a crisis. Moses was actually her third child. When Moses was born he had a 9 year old sister and a brother about 3. Jochebed is introduced in the book of Exodus, chapter two. Her story of persistence follows Shiphrah and Puah, the Hebrew midwives who feared God. In an earlier chapter we learned they modeled what fearing the Lord looks like.

The midwives **S**erved God, **L**oved God, **O**bserved His Commands, and **W**alked in all His Ways. They chose to do the right thing, no matter what. Shiphrah and Puah refused to do as the Pharaoh commanded: to kill all baby boys born in the O.B. Department of the Hebrew camp. Instead, they were prepared not to fall to pieces should a crisis come and chose to obey God and follow His ways.

Pharaoh's first two plans of destroying the Israelites failed. He needed another plan.

Plan #3 - kill all baby boys by throwing them into the river.

Exodus 1:22 (NIV) "The Pharaoh gave this order to all his people: "Every boy that is born you must throw into the Nile, but let every girl live."

Pharaoh's second attempt at stopping this nation from growing failed because of two gutsy women. These two gutsy and God fearing women were a part of the nation of Israel. This nation was in bondage in Egypt. Pharaoh was concerned, scared really, of how strong the nation was becoming by the number of people that kept growing this fruitful nation.

You see, God had promised His people the Israelites they would be fruitful and multiply. Remember, God is a covenant God. He keeps His Word. If God said it, it will happen. It looked as if Pharaoh was intimidated by Israel's rapid growth as a nation, when in actuality he was intimidated by Israel's God.

As an intimidated, scared leader, Pharaoh was obsessed with stopping the Hebrew people from growing and his obsession led him to act in preposterous, murderous ways. Actually he was nothing but a wimp. Obviously! He demanded that two women do his bidding. Instead, God assigned those two women; two gutsy, persistent women, to intimidate this wimpy, scared king.

His third plan of ordering others to kill baby boys is another example of his cowardice. And this coward has no idea that his plan will backfire on him. It will take years for the outcome of this backfire to become evident.

The firestorm of this pending backfire is another persistent woman: a woman *who is firmly & stubbornly determined to maintain a purpose through persistence.* A woman steadfast in her purpose: to save her child. She is pregnant, she is an Israelite, and she is aware of the Pharaoh's edict. But she's a strong willed, persistent woman. Look out Pharaoh! Here she comes.

This story unfolds in Exodus 2:1-10. And it's a true story. It really happened. When we refer to things we read in the Bible as *stories* we need to be careful we don't think of them like a work of fiction. Bible stories come straight out of God's Word. That makes them truth. They are His-stories, His-story, history; therefore, fact.

Noah and his ark truly happened. Jonah inside the belly of a fish truly happened. Daniel in a den of lions, untouched and safe, truly happened. A shepherd boy took down a giant, with one smooth stone, it truly happened. A baby boy was born to a virgin, it truly happened. A blind man's sight is restored by spit mixed with dirt, it truly happened. A daughter was pronounced dead but she woke up, that, too, truly happened. And a man, dead, was inside his tomb for three days and when Jesus shouted his name he walked out. It truly happened. True, real life stories. In God's Word.

Here in Exodus chapter 2 we're introduced to Jochebed, a real-life, determined, strong willed, persistent woman who refused to fall to pieces in her crisis. When she realized she was pregnant she did all she could to protect the child within. Exodus 2:2 tells us she hid the baby for three months after he was born. I believe we can assume she hid the entire pregnancy as well.

This same verse even tells us she "saw that he was a fine child." Other places in the Bible refer to him as "no ordinary child." God's hand was on this boy from the beginning. God moved in this woman's heart. God made her persistent and then used her persistence to bring His plan and His purpose to fruition. God had plans for Moses. God was ready to lead His people out of Egypt and He hand-picked Moses to do it. God also hand-picked this woman to be the mother of this future deliverer of God's people. Jochebed was in persistent-mode from the moment she knew she was pregnant.

Imagine being Jochebed. She lived in bondage. She was a slave in Egypt. All the Israelites were slaves. And things were getting worse. Pharaoh's first plan was to work this nation so hard that they wouldn't be able to grow in numbers. His second plan was to use the midwives to make sure all baby boys were killed as soon as they were born on the delivery stool. As a woman she would have been very aware of her monthly cycle and like the other Hebrew women perhaps they stayed away from their husbands so as to not conceive during their fertile time of the month.

But as many people know, planning when to have children or how many to have is a little harder than it sounds. I should know! Of my four biological children three were conceived on some form of birth control, including the pill. We planned to wait five years to have kids, but we had four children within five years.

Exodus 2 (NIV): *2 and she became pregnant and gave birth to a son. When she saw that he was a fine child, she hid him for three months.*

As soon as Jochebed knew she was pregnant she went into persistent mode. Before her son was born she already had thought through some of her ideas. Prior to her crisis she had done some research, some reconnaissance, an examination of the area followed by detailed surveying. She was a woman prepared and her persistence propelled her to plan. How did she hide her growing belly? Did she go to the midwives, Shiphrah and Puah, for this birth? We're not sure of this particular detail but based on what happens next we know she planned, we know she was persistent.

When her baby boy was born she continued planning. We can assume she was wise with each detail. For instance, she had two other children in the house. How did they not spill the beans on the fact that they had a baby brother? Seeing as this family lived in bondage, their living conditions would have been rather small, in close confines of their neighbors. How did Jochebed keep a baby quiet? Did he scream? Did he suffer with colic?

Scripture doesn't fill these blanks in for us but we can read between the lines and see it would not have been easy to keep a baby hidden for three months. Not easy, but definitely do-able, with persistence as the guide. Exodus 2:2 tells us she did it!

Exodus 2 (NIV): [3] *But when she could hide him no longer, she got a papyrus basket for him and coated it with tar and pitch. Then she placed the child in it and put it among the reeds along the bank of the Nile.* [4] *His sister stood at a distance to see what would happen to him.*

Her next persistent plan is laid out. She makes a basket. (Dang! She's a resourceful, persistent, AND creative woman.) She thinks of everything. She makes a basket that will carry her son in water so he will be safe. She even includes her older daughter in the plan.

Exodus 2 (NIV): [5] *Then Pharaoh's daughter went down to the Nile to bathe, and her attendants were walking along the river bank. She saw the basket among the reeds and sent her slave girl to get it.* [6] *She opened it and saw the baby. He was crying, and she felt sorry for him. "This is one of the Hebrew babies," she said.* [7] *Then his sister asked Pharaoh's daughter, "Shall I go and get one of the Hebrew women to nurse the baby for you?"*

Ok. So Jochebed *just happens* to place her baby in the river when the princess, the Pharoah's daughter, *just happens* to be bathing and Jochebed's daughter *just happens* to show up at the exact moment when the baby is recognized as a Hebrew baby and then the little girl *just happens* to offer to get a Hebrew woman to nurse the baby?

Really? Seriously? Are you not ecstatic with how this whole plan is unfolding? You should be! I can hardly sit still over these kinds of things when I'm studying the Bible. This is what makes reading and studying the Word of God incredible. Seeing His hand orchestrate the unbelievable, the miraculous, and the incredible plans written throughout His Word should make us overjoyed, thrilled, excited! I can hardly contain myself when God reveals what we may see as coincidence but it's really Him coordinating circumstances and in control.

Jochebed is watching this whole plan unfold. She's hidden behind the reeds at the bank of the river. She's like the movie director, perched on top of his tall chair watching the many-times rehearsed scene finally being filmed. Only Jochebed has not rehearsed this scene. Oh, she's rehearsed it in her mind, alright, over and over, I'm sure. But she only had one shot at this elaborate plan taking place perfectly, flawlessly, exactly, as she had planned.

Exodus 2 (NIV): *8 "Yes, go," she answered. And the girl went and got the baby's mother. 9 Pharaoh's daughter said to her, "Take this baby and nurse him for me, and I will pay you." So the woman took the baby and nursed him. 10 When the child grew older, she took him to Pharaoh's daughter and he became her son. She named him Moses, saying, "I drew him out of the water."*

What?!?! Did you catch all that? The baby's sister, though the Princess was clueless about that tidbit, went and got a Hebrew mother (the baby's actual mother, another piece missed by the princess) to take the baby....*take the baby*...back to her home, *her home*, and nurse him and care for him until the child was weaned. AND SHE WOULD GET PAID!

Paid to take care of her own flesh and blood. Surely this had never happened in over 400 years, since the Israelite people were in Egypt, a slave was paid to keep her own son. Seeing as children were most likely weaned off their mother's breast at about five years of age, she indeed kept her son, cared for her son, for years.

Here's persistence in action. This strong willed woman schemed and planned and didn't really disobey the Pharaoh's edict. How's that? Exodus 1:22 (NIV) says, "Every boy that is born you must throw into the Nile." She did. Ok, she didn't actually throw or cast, fling or hurl the baby as the literal meaning says, but into the Nile the baby boy went.

This Hebrew baby grew up in the Pharaoh's palace with purpose. He would one day be called by God to be the deliverer of God's people. Moses would one day lead the nation of Israel right out of bondage. He would lead over one million people out of their chains, walk them out of their bondage. Moses was used by God as He had always intended, because a persistent woman refused to fall to pieces in her crisis.

She is a role model to me.

After Kevin and I returned from our weekend away, after the diagnosis in November, we went to the appointment with the gynecologic oncologist. He concurred with the original findings from Dr. H and a plan was set in motion.

We were inundated with information, schedules, descriptions, definitions, a plan of action for my surgery and treatments. A plan that unfolded over the course of about six months.

Surgery was scheduled with a complete hysterectomy, removal of 14 lymph nodes and pelvic washings. A longer stay at the hospital was required. Though I will not go into all the details surrounding those few weeks there were many complications along the way. A compromised nerve in my leg after the removal of lymph nodes that to this day still causes some minor leg mobility issues. An all out fainting episode in the shower the day I returned home post surgery.

Another required hospital stay with a surgical procedure to drain a hematoma (an internal collection of blood) that was causing me pain and fevers. Multiple bladder infections. The list goes on.

Challenges came my way. Crises within the crisis stacked up. Opportunities to fall to pieces presented themselves. Persistence was a must for this woman!

At that first appointment, the oncologist's nurse went through a lot of important information with us, including the side effects of the upcoming chemotherapy. She caught my attention a little more as she mentioned hair loss as one of those effects. I like my hair.

I don't mean I like the fact that I have hair, I mean, that I really enjoy my hair. I like changing the colors and the highlights often. I enjoy my hair. I love having the style changed as well. Our family has moved a number of times over the past 25 years. Since turning 21, I've personally lived in over 15 different dwellings, 9 different communities. That means having to change doctors and dentists 9 different times.

That also requires needing to find a different hairstylist each time. I'd rather look for a doctor. Finding the right hair stylist is not an easy task. Don't get me wrong, I'm not a woman who is obsessed with my external appearance. What I look like doesn't define who I am. I just like having cute hair. That's all.

When the nurse brought up the topic of hair loss she said something like, "There's over a 98% chance your hair will fall out." Naturally I took that to mean there's a 2% chance it wouldn't.

But it did. You may be asking yourself, "What does persistence have to do with hair loss?" Well, for me, everything! I was *firmly & stubbornly determined to maintain a purpose through persistence.* I was determined to not fall to pieces in my crisis.

Did I like the thought of losing my hair? Absolutely not!

Was I looking forward to having my hair cut super-duper short so when it fell out it wasn't so dramatic for me? Absolutely not!

Was I emotionally prepared for the moment when I woke up in the middle of the night, scratched my head and ended up with a handful of super-duper short blonde hair? Absolutely not!

Was I prepared for not shaving legs and armpits for months? No.

Did I notice that not needing to wash my hair or shave my legs made for a very short shower? Of course, but I still didn't like it!

Was I surprised that my eyelashes and eyebrows fell out? Yes.

Does that translate to uh-oh-she-fell-to-pieces-in-her-hair-loss-crisis? Absolutely not!

Being hurt, upset, emotionally tired, worn out, frustrated, sad, confused, or unsure does not translate to, "Look out, she's about to fall to pieces." Hating my hair loss, missing my hair, and disliking wearing hats were not falling to pieces. Rather, it was hating hair loss, missing my hair, and disliking wearing hats; plain and simple.

To this day I am reminded every morning when I curl my eyelashes that I had cancer. Prior to cancer I never had to curl my eyelashes. Never. They grew dark and naturally curled in an upward direction. When my eyelashes grew back they grew straight. I don't get it and I don't like it. However, I have a choice on how I will perceive this inconvenience.

I choose to be reminded of God's grace, of His tender loving care to me in my crisis. Each time I grab the eyelash curler I remember God's assignment to me. Every single time I curl my eyelashes I am reminded and I recognize God's Hand on my life.

At the time of this crisis we had been living in that community for about seven years; the longest we had lived anywhere since Kevin and I had been married. As I reflect back, it is no coincidence God planted us there that long. It took time to become part of the community and of a church family the way we did. The roots we planted went deep and we were blessed to be on our crisis journey in such a loving and caring community.

The hair stylist I had at that time was simply put, a gift. One day in November, right after my diagnosis, I was in her chair as she was doing her craft on my head. Seemingly out of nowhere, but actually, out of agape love, she asked a tough question. She went right to the point. She didn't mince words, she didn't stumble on her words, and she didn't pre-apologize for what was about to come out of her mouth.

The words she spoke were like smooth, rich, creamy dark chocolate sauce to my ears. Some would say honey but I hate honey so I changed the analogy to suit my preference. Probably more proof of my strong will: changing a decades-old analogy to suit my own desire.

Here's what she said, "Hey, Ellen, when you begin to lose your hair, would you like me to shave your head?"

There it was. The intimidating matter that had been securely shut in a dark place in my mind, a matter that was being ignored, was now opened and light was shed on it because my hair stylist had guts to bring up the tough subject. For me, that moment urged me into a persistent mode that remained for months. I was dreading losing my hair. Her words steadied the dread. Her gutsy determination, her persistence, helped me to accept what was coming even if I still wasn't very happy about it. I was now able to now talk about it, even plan for it. Her persistence helped me along my journey in dealing with my hair loss crisis.

One day, my eldest child, Christine and I went to a local shop/spa that specializes in providing care to women who are undergoing cancer treatment and will experience hair loss. I was in plan-mode, thanks to my gutsy hairstylist, so we spent a good part of the day there.

I wasn't sure if I wanted a wig or not. It was winter in Michigan. Hair is a natural furnace for the head, especially with the amount of hairspray I use. I wondered if wearing a wig would help to keep my head warm.

Our goal for the day was to decide what to do for head coverings when the inevitable happened. As I left the place I knew one thing: no wig for me. I just couldn't find a comfortable option, one that made me at ease. Don't get me wrong, I tried oodles of options. Christine and I actually had a blast that day. We laughed; we were silly. I was a red head, a brunette. I experienced curly hair and long straight hair. I tried on more than fifteen wigs, none were for me. All was good, though. I left the shop with a plan...and a few hats and head coverings for what was to come. Persistence made a plan.

There was one time right after treatments were done Christine and I, along with one of my sisters, my niece and, my mom all went on a girl's day out. We shopped, ate lunch, giggled...we had a fun day all around. We went in all kinds of shops we would never purchase anything from, we just decided to window shop from both sides of the window. Since I didn't have any hair I found it intriguing to look at all sorts of head coverings.

We walked in one store and somehow a mannequin was bumped and nearly tipped over. Of course that caused all kinds of attempted suppressed laughter as we fumbled trying to put the mannequin upright. Much to my delight, this plastic person we had nearly toppled over was wearing a wig. A huge fluffy head of white hair was perched on the top of this mannequin.

I was suddenly compelled to see what I would look like with huge, fluffy, white, out-of-control hair. Persistence allowed me to enjoy life, even laugh at certain times over what could have potentially been a struggle.

Persistence laughs

Due to my gutsy hair stylists' question about shaving my head I even had a plan just in case I'm in the 98% window and my hair does fall out. Did I want to have her shave my head? The answer to the question was, "Yes, I did." She would shave my head once my hair started falling out. All I had to do was call Jen when I needed her. Her clippers and her agape love would be ready.

January 26, 2010 was the day it happened. I woke up in the early hours of the morning, scratched my head, and ended up with a tuft of hair in my hands. I woke Kevin up and he held me while I cried. He gently asked what I was going to do. This persistent, though crying woman laid out her plan to her man. Because I had a plan to tell him. Because persistence plans.

The plan unfolded WAY better than I could have hoped or had even dreamed possible.

Weeks earlier a friend, a center-of-the-bull's-eye-kind-of-friend, had called and asked if she could come for a visit. We made a date for January 26. At the time, I had no idea what this day would hold for me. When I went to bed the night before I had decided to put a pot of soup on early the next day so Wendy and I could spend a large portion of the day just sitting in the living room, visiting. That was this persistent woman's plan. God added to that plan.

It should not come as a surprise to me that Wendy was preplanned to come to my house that day. It just wasn't a coincidence that the exact day I would begin to lose my hair, was the same day Wendy was coming for a visit.

I didn't plan that. On my best day I couldn't plan that well. God knew what I needed, when I needed it. He planned for Wendy to come that day. And she was the perfect person to show up on the very day my hair was falling out.

Before Wendy had knocked on my door, I had called Jen and arranged to go to her house later that morning for the shaving of my head. God beat me to it.

It was a Tuesday. Jen is always busy on Tuesdays. She always had clients pre-booked on Tuesdays. But not this Tuesday. This Tuesday all of her appointments were vacant. Not one scheduled appointment in her day. Add that to the fact that I was only able to call and make this appointment because she had previously opened that very difficult dark place for me. God certainly showed up before and during this hair crisis.

Wendy came mid-morning. We hugged and then sat on the couch and began chit-chatting. Now you must know that Wendy is the kind of friend that is fun to be around. Every moment spent with Wendy in the past involved a whole lot of fun and laughter...the kind of laughter that, well, let's just say that I'm really glad I had a particular procedure done so that laughing is not always accompanied by, "Excuse me, I must go to the bathroom for a moment."

Wendy is known for her ability to make people laugh. She is also deeply caring and ready to discuss spiritual matters for long periods of time. Our day would have been filled with various topics and emotions. After our initial chit-chatting, I asked, with no transition or segue at all, "So I need to have my head shaved today, wanna go with?"

Her response? Well, before I mention that, I want to make sure you really understand Wendy. She is funny. She is caring. And she is also always ready for an adventure.

So when I blurted out my question to her, she immediately replied, "Oh my gosh! That would be so much fun!" This exclamation from Wendy in no way reveals an uncaring response. Wendy is deeply compassionate and sympathetic. But she's like me, spontaneous at times. And that's what drove that response out of her mouth.

And it was the exact answer I needed!!

God had placed another persistent woman in my life at just the exact moment I needed her. My emotions were in commotion. God knew that. He knew it ahead of time. He knew it at the beginning of time. So He placed Wendy on my calendar that day.

Off to Jen's we went. It was an adventure I will never forget. It was filled with tears, laughter, cameras, creativity, spontaneity and yes, even joy, as I sat in Jen's chair and experienced a day I still treasure. These two gutsy women helped me to not fall to pieces in my crisis. They were my Shiphrah & Puah, my splendor and beauty, for that day.

Before Jen began shaving, the three of us huddled together, held hands, and Wendy prayed. Peace flooded my soul.

Jen turned on her clippers and began her work. I immediately stopped her. I said the day held spontaneity. Without missing a beat I asked if she could 'carve' something in the back of my head. I am the mom who NEVER let her boys engrave any number, symbol, or sign as an opportunity to show off team spirit on their athletic heads. If asked, I would respond, "Absolutely not!!!" But I was about to go against my own rule.

"I can try," she replied. "What are you thinking?"

"I want 16:5 engraved on the back of my head." I wanted a constant reminder of my assignment. She turned her clippers back on. Wendy spontaneously interrupted and asked if she could shave a Mohawk on the top of my head. Well, that began all kinds of mischievous interactions. And laughter.

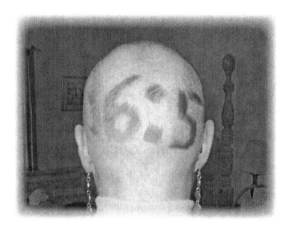

Psalm 16:5, my assignment reminder

I later learned that Wendy needed to step out of the salon a couple of times because she needed to "pull herself together." It is no easy task to watch your friend go through a crisis and she needed to have her moments of emotional unrest, as well. But the whole time she never once wavered from her persistence to be a support to me. She and Jen later shared that though we had fun, the day was especially difficult for each of them. I appreciate these two persistent women at a new level because of it. Persistence, from them to me, was a treasured moment.

After my head was shaved I had whiskers all over my head. Little tiny whiskers everywhere. When I laid my head on the pillow it felt like pins sticking me in the head. If I tried to pluck them out with the ends of my fingers they would come out without any discomfort or feeling at all. If I tried to rub my head with my hands in an attempt to make a lot come out at one time it was a complete failure. Nothing happened. It didn't make sense to me...plucking brought success but a very slow-go. Rubbing would have worked much faster but to no avail. Ugh!

Between being bald and having whiskers all over my head that felt like mini daggers going into my skull and catching on my hats like a hang nail on pantyhose, I was frustrated, irritated, and discouraged.

I needed an attitude adjustment. Or as I referred to it at that time, a *hat-titude adjustment.* When I look back in my journal from this journey I notice I shared some frustrations, I was honest in my doubts. Wait. A woman who refuses to fall to pieces in a crisis doubts? Perhaps. I know I did.

And God made sure He met me where I needed Him. My pastor (my hubby) has shared a familiar phrase for many years now. He says, "God loves you right where you are but He loves you too much to leave you there." I doubted, and God still loved me right there. In my doubt, God loved me. But, He loved me too much to leave me there. He would speak His truth into me through the reading of His Word. He would speak His truth into me through people, a song, a card. The avenues which our God uses are endless. He meets us and we respond, even if there's no response, in reality even that is a response.

How did God love me right where I was? Very creatively.

He loved me right where I was at as my whisker issues were taking a great deal of my emotional strength. A few days after being shaved I was in my bathroom applying my makeup when I had this incredibly, creative, ingenious thought.

I am not a genius, so I know this was God *loving me right where I was at…*right in my bathroom, and sharing His creativity with me as a way of *loving me too much to leave me there.*

One minute I was discouraged from the whiskers and the next minute I was grabbing the lint roller. You know, the roller with the adhesive masking tape on it. I began rolling that adhesive tape roller all over my head. In no time at all I had filled the sticky paper with whiskers.

I did it again. In no time I had another loaded-with-whiskers sticky piece of paper. Once again I was overwhelmed by how tenderly my Lord cares for His children.

Matthew 10:30 (NIV) "And even the very hairs on your head are all numbered." The thought of God keeping count of the hairs on my head even as He had been subtracting hair for days since it began falling out caused me to smile. After all, He would now have to do some pretty quick math as He totaled how many hairs landed on the sticky paper every time I swiped it back and forth on my head.

I went to the main floor of our house, found Kevin and told him of my latest discovery regarding the lint roller. I asked him, "Please, would you lint roll my head?" He looked at me as if I had grown another head. I pleaded again. He acquiesced. He cautiously approached this new concept but he began rolling. And it didn't take long for him to have a new *role* in my crisis.

I'll let you in on a secret. When Kevin and I were engaged we practiced the wedding kiss. *Sure ya did (wink, wink).* We actually did. We practiced for the mere fact that we didn't want it to just be any ordinary kiss. We wanted to remember it as a special connection; not just a whew-it's-over-now-let's-go-eat-some-cake kind of moment. Or a let's-give-'em-something-to-really-whoop-and-holler-over. We wanted it to be our moment, one we would look back on and remember. A kiss that sealed the deal. A kiss that when crises in our marriage happen we could remember what sealed the covenant we had just made in front of hundreds of people.

The kiss. *The* kiss is one of the highlights of my wedding day. It was an extraordinary, emphasis on the *extra*-ordinary, kiss. As the pastor asked Kevin if he was ready to kiss his bride, Kevin took his time. He looked me in the eye and at that moment it seemed like hundreds of people disappeared. It was as if we were the only two people in that sanctuary. My groom gently placed his hands on my cheeks, while looking into my eyes. He cupped my face with his strong hands, tilted his head, and gave me a very tender kiss that said, "What I just vowed to God about you in front of all these witnesses, I meant it, I seal it now!"

So twenty one years later we were standing in our bathroom as he was lint rolling my head then he placed the lint roller on the counter and began rubbing my bald head with his bare hands. I knew we were about to have another moment to remember, similar to the one we had at the altar on September 24, 1988. He gently, tenderly began rubbing my bald head. Then he placed kisses all over his bald wife's head. After that, he put both of his safe, big hands on each side of my head (I could even feel the cold of his wedding band touching my bare scalp) and he kissed me; a gentle, *extra*ordinary, kiss. In my mind I went back twenty one years and heard his voice say, "I DO" when asked if he would love, honor, cherish, and keep in *sickness and in health.*

That moment alone put a huge deposit in my persistence bank. That moment filled me. My husband showed me that our marriage would not to fall to pieces in our crisis. He made a vow to God and he would keep that vow. Kevin helped my hat-titude to be purposeful; he encouraged my hat-titude to allow others to see the Christ through the persistence in my crisis.

Kevin and I with a purposeful hat-titude

Easter 2010

CHAPTER 6

Provision through the Crisis

The Sunday before my first chemo treatment my pastor (who, I might add, is ridiculously handsome) preached a message about manna, an unexpected help or aid. Provision from God. Manna.

I wrote in my journal about this particular sermon and mentioned that since hearing it I began to pay closer attention to the unexpected gifts, the provision, in my crisis. I began to view them as my manna. I wrote in one entry, *Manna showed up in a lime green and pink bag today. Manna poured out....HATS!!! Beautiful, cute, stylish, classy, hats. I was overwhelmed. A dear sister in the Lord had walked her cancer journey a couple of years prior to me and she was allowing me to borrow her hats.* Manna, for this persistent woman, who didn't want to wear a wig.

Manna poured down on me at so many times during my crisis. God's unexpected help or aid was noticed often. It was impressed on me, through my husband's sermon, to take note of God's provision as manna so that the *unexpected help or aid* wouldn't get included with or mistaken for the everyday, normal, regular happenings. For instance, a card in the mail was manna, not a nice person sending a nice card. A meal prepared by a caring person was manna, not someone just being thoughtful.

Manna poured down! I paid closer attention to the cards, the meals prepared by others, volunteers to help cook, clean, and iron. Each instance became more than a favor or a friendly act or gesture.

I held the prayer shawl close, I wrapped up in the fleece blanket, I treasured each piece of jewelry gifted to me during my crisis. I valued the books, the music, and other gifts I received. I cherished the visitors at my chemo injections. They all became more than gifts; they were manna, my manna, my unexpected provision from God in my crisis.

Mom and sisters are my manna for a chemo treatment

Kevin and I love to go on vacation once a year, by ourselves, to a warm place, always at the beach. Just the two of us. If we go as a family, it's an adventure; if it's just my husband and I then it's a vacation.

Right after I got diagnosed and knew the treatments, chemo plus radiation, would be over by April we began planning the *celebration vacation after radiation somewhere in the nation by some form of transportation*. Silly, I know, but it gave me a sense of hope. Even something so silly as that phrase was manna to me.

We knew the diagnosis, the treatments, the whole crisis would have us emotionally spent so having a *celebration vacation after radiation* in our sights gave us something to look forward to; something to give us energy and focus. Did that mean I was close to falling to pieces in my crisis? No. It meant I was excited to go on a vacation with my man after having to go through some difficult chemo treatments and radiation.

Celebration Vacation After Radiation

Radiation. One of the worst parts of this crisis. The radiation treatment I had is called HDR radiation, an acronym for high dose rate radiation. To any medical person reading this, forgive me as I describe this in laymen's terms.

The radiation I had was done internally so I went a total of five times and received a high dose of radiation. Seeing as it's given internally it can be given at a much higher dose because it doesn't have tissue to go through and potentially damage. It's an internal radiation. My oncologist and the radiologist did a great job of describing and explaining what I would experience while undergoing the treatments. And yet, I still didn't grasp precisely what would happen until I was actually experiencing it first-hand.

If I were asked, "What was the closest you came to falling to pieces in your crisis?" I would have to answer, "During radiation." Being 'close to' falling to pieces and actually falling to pieces are two different things. It's similar to Humpty Dumpty in the introduction of this book. While on the edge of the wall, close to falling, Humpty was good, there was no damage done. However, when Humpty Dumpty went over the edge, he fell, he broke. I was *close* to falling to pieces, but I didn't fall.

Radiation was a struggle for me. And here's where I must apologize before as I give detailed information about this experience. Apologize for being detailed? No, apologize for what the particular details are. Keeping in mind I had *internal* radiation and that can only be applied one way. *Internally.* I will attempt to be careful how I describe things, but I will also make sure you get a good idea of what I experienced; therefore, details matter. Why? Because it's a part of my journey, and how I learned more about God's provision, His manna, to me in this particular crisis called radiation.

Each time radiation was given a time of preparation was necessary. The preparation required a CT scan of the area needing the radiation so that the Nuclear Physicist could pinpoint exactly where the radiation must go and create a plan of action for the five minute actual dispensing of the treatment. Due to the treatment being done internally, there is no room for error. In other words, you wouldn't want the wrong area, the wrong parts, receiving radiation.

Now the CT scan itself was no big deal. How I was prepared for the scan was a big deal. All clothing from the waist down is removed. I was flat on my back on what they refer to as a bed. I'll call it the long, thin slab of metal not designed for anyone over 100 pounds...where I'm only supposed to be for about 20-ish minutes. (The first time I was on the metal slab for almost two hours due to some glitches.) This is where I get detailed.

As I said, I was laid on the slab, but I was also strapped down to the very uncomfortable 'bed'. Don't get the idea that I was strapped down by belts around my legs and midsection. No, I was strapped down by a contraption that was between my legs and hooked to something that was, let's just say, to save my dignity and your discomfort, I was attached to the same instrument that was used to dispense the radiation that would be given *internally.*

Some of you are grasping the idea right away and some of you are going to take a little longer. Let's just say, I was uncomfortable, in more ways than one, to say the least. Keep in mind I couldn't move a centimeter or the radiation would do permanent damage, so the *strapping down* was extremely secure, yet essential. AND... more than one person took a close look at how the contraption was inserted, attached, and whether the board was straight or not; yup - an intact dignity was a challenge for me.

How exactly did manna rain down in this part of my crisis? Well, honestly, I had to have a reality check for this manna-finding when I returned home later that day and after the elaborate pity party where only three people were invited: me, myself, and I. How did God provide in this awful experience? Manna came in a variety of ways but I was unable to see them when I was focused on the awfulness of the experience. When I took my eyes off of me and my circumstance, I was able to see His manna in my crisis.

A dear friend, Jan, offered to go with me to this first radiation appointment. As we arrived at our destination Jan stopped me in the parking lot, took my hands in hers, and prayed before going any further. Manna. As I reflected back on that day God showed me He provided a sense of peace. How? As I was strapped to the slab-o-metal knowing a friend was in the waiting room brought a sense of peace. As I left the experience I was greeted by her friendly, smiling face and her compassionate concern. The ride home wasn't terrible and lonely because she was paying close attention to my mood and intentionally meeting my emotional needs. Manna.

I must be honest here. When I heard a Nuclear Physicist was involved in my radiation therapy, I automatically stereotyped. Now if you've earned this title, Nuclear Physicist, or any other -*icist*, I do not mean any disrespect. I actually have a great deal of respect for your determination and intelligence. However, the first thought I had when the person responsible for my radiation was referred to as a Nuclear Physicist was "geek."

To me, this is a term of endearment. You see, I gave birth to a geek. My oldest child is a geek. Not because she's a nuclear physicist, but because of her determination and her intelligence. She was the valedictorian of her high school, she scored *really* high, ridiculously high, on her college entrance exam, and her lowest grade *ever* is an A-, which she received in one class during college. She's a geek. Although she has my DNA I'm still really confused on how I contributed to any of her geek-ability.

The physicist assigned to me was a beautiful woman; she clearly had brains, but she was also pretty, out-going, and friendly. Brains, looks, nice figure, AND a personality? Yeah, she had all that, but more importantly, she was kind, compassionate, and attentive. It didn't matter at all what she looked like and it didn't matter at all that her title ended with *icist*. What truly mattered was that she cared and she showed it in my time of crisis. That was MANNA to me.

The people who *lovingly* (that might include a tiny bit of sarcasm) attached me to the slab-o-metal were patient, caring, and friendly. They even sensed my disposition and at times said something silly to lighten the atmosphere, to cut through the aura of anxiety. We actually spoke of cute shoes and I would say, "Oooo, I like those earrings" and they would say something like, "You look so cute in that bandana," which was my popular choice of headwear at those appointments. More manna.

Simple kindness, a heartfelt compliment spoken at just the right moment, friendly, smiling faces from people who have a difficult job all contributed to this unexpected aid. Each person in this strenuous and challenging place contributed to the manna raining down on me. Provision in my crisis.

Manna showed up one day in the tanning salon. Really, Ellen? Yes, indeed, it did.

Since Kevin & I were anticipating our celebration-vacation-after-radiation, I decided to get a head start on my tan by going to a local tanning salon. A huge part of the enjoyment of a vacation with Kevin is sitting side-by-side on the beach reading, napping, watching the waves hit the shore, feeling the sand in-between our toes or walking on the beach.

As I was waiting for a bed at the local tanning salon an acquaintance noticed me standing in line. We didn't know each other well, just one of those first-name-basis people. We knew each other from a few places around town. Our kids played sports together, years earlier I had worked at a local coffee shop and she would frequent that establishment. Her family owned and operated a local, thriving business that I would patron occasionally. We knew each other enough to inquire with a, "How are you?" and the acceptable, but vague, response, "Fine, and you?" She's one of those women I appreciate who always has a smile and a pleasant disposition.

Had someone not known that I was going through cancer treatments it wouldn't take a genius (like my daughter or the physicist) to figure out. One look at my eyebrow-less/eyelash-less face and my bandana-sportin'-head and you'd have the choices narrowed down. She figured it out. This acquaintance walked into the tanning salon, headed in my direction, and said, "Oh, Ellen, I am so sorry. I didn't know. Where is your cancer?"

I loved that moment. I loved that she came right to the point, right there in that tanning salon. I gave her the revised edition, included the celebration-vacation as the reason I was at the tanner and she said she'd be praying for me and we said our goodbyes. More manna. More unexpected aid providing a smile in my day.

Later that same night I was already in my bedroom, resting, when a knock came at the front door. I heard one of my sons answer the door and say, "I sure will, have a good night and thank you." A minute later that son was in my bedroom handing me an envelope.

As I opened the card I immediately saw it was from the lady, the friendly acquaintance from the tanning salon. Inside the envelope was a beautiful hand-written note of encouragement with a sizeable cash gift included. The note explained that I was to spend the money while on that celebration vacation. I was to buy something I would never purchase for myself. The note was a kind 'demand' that I pamper and spoil myself. An unexpected gift. Manna.

I had never received a gift like that before, especially from someone who wasn't even on the bull's eye of friendships. I was overwhelmed. By the amount of cash? Sure, but that's not all. I was amazed, once again, by the manna that had fallen on me in such an unexpected way. Provision, from an unlikely source.

Our God is so good and so creative and He loves lavishing that goodness and creativity on His children. I am more amazed by the goodness from our good God than I am the gifts and surprises from people. He continues to surprise His children. He continues to lavish His goodness on His children because He loves His children. His manna is extensive. His manna is sufficient. His manna shows up at just the right time. It's never early. It's never late.

This next piece of manna is what I refer to as my *Manna Madness to my Momma's Heart*. My son, Troy, had an assignment in his 9th grade English class shortly after my treatments were completed. This was my manna that spring day in May 2010:

MY SURVIVOR

My mom was assigned cancer in Dec of 2009. She is also the strongest woman I know, not just mentally, but physically too. Nobody wants her to have cancer, but she has it. It was difficult for my mom to accept the fact she had cancer. Even through all this she stayed positive, and loving. She had a loving family to back her up. My mom has had to tell her children and her parents. It took a lot of emotional strength to tell us.

My mom can do a lot. She had to tell her kids she had cancer. Saying this to her children broke her down. It was hard to see her high school & college aged children cry. My brothers & I were wondering why her. The news made everyone weak, especially my parents. Nobody in my family thought in a million years something like this would hit so close to home. Almost anyone else would be negative, but my mom remained positive through all of it.

If it was tough for my mom to tell my siblings and me, then I don't know how to describe how hard it was for her to tell her parents. To tell the people that have loved and raised you for so long that you have cancer, would be the worst thing in the world. Also, she had to see her mom's reaction and watch her cry. The sorrow at my house sounded like it could be at a funeral, but no one died.

I don't know about you, but when I hear the word surgery, I cringe. I hate that word. It has a good outcome but never feels good after. My mom had to get a very difficult surgery done. She was sore for weeks. It was very difficult for her to get up and walk to the bathroom. My dad had to help around the house. When she sat down she randomly had pains throughout her body. It was a burden for the whole family to see our mom and wife suffer so much. Throughout the whole experience we had an attitude like "why her, why our mom?" My mom persevered though. She remained strong through the whole hardship. She never gave up hope, or gave up God.

Nobody should have to go through cancer treatment. Chemo wiped my mom out. She felt horrible and couldn't do a whole lot. My mom wasn't able to go to some basketball games and sometimes she couldn't go to church. It hurt for her to stand up and sit down. She couldn't get comfortable no matter what she did. My mom also lost one of her best friends, her hair. She loved that poofy stuff so much. Even though she hurt inside she didn't always show like some people. She said, "Hey, now I can't have a bad hair day" and went on with life. She could have just gave up but she persevered through it all.

My mom is the most beautiful, strong, loving person I know. She can fight and stay positive through anything life throws at her. She didn't even let cancer break her down, she rose above it. My mom used cancer to preach to people. She tells them that everyone will have a hardship. As long as you pray and have loving people to back you up, you will get through it. My mom also says that everyone is assigned an assignment by God. She stayed strong and positive through her assignment and passed. Will you pass your assignment?

By: Troy Harbin

Provision, manna, came to me in unexpected ways at unexpected times in my crisis. I love all the original, creative, ingenious ways God provided for me. He knew what I needed at just the time I needed it. And He provided the persons and the means, to make sure each particular piece of manna fell in my direction, on my life, in the middle of my crisis as a way to help me not fall to pieces in my crisis. I thank Him that He gave me eyes to see His manna as it poured down on me. Manna, as His provision in my crisis.

CHAPTER 7

Power over the Crisis

Have you ever considered who from the Bible you'd like to have lunch with? Who you would love to chat with over your favorite cup of coffee? There are so many women in the Bible who I can't wait to meet face-to-face. I would be so excited to do lunch with some of the women who have been great examples of how to live, how to do the right thing no matter what.

I imagine that attempting to connect with Mary, the mother of Jesus, for a lunch date or even a cup of coffee may be difficult since she's one of the more well-known women warriors of Scripture. Jochebed or Shiphrah & Puah, now their schedules may be a tad more available.

But there is definitely one woman I want to meet; a lady who, in my opinion, had an immense amount of guts and boldness, and she's one of my favorites to teach on, to speak about, and to share with others.

If you've ever felt insignificant, like you go unnoticed, or that you aren't worth noticing, this woman is one you'll want to get to know. Maybe you'll connect to her right away just by knowing this one fact about her: she's unnamed. She's one of my biblical heroes and her name is never mentioned. Perhaps her name was Mary, like 987 other women in the New Testament, and to avoid any confusion that's why she's left unnamed. (I wish you could hear the way I would say this part out loud. If you could, you'd find that it's laced with a little sarcasm and humor.)

This woman's story is told in Mark 5:25. I really like reading the KJV, the King James Version on this verse, *"And a certain woman, which had an issue of blood twelve years..."*

This unnamed woman and I have something in common. We both had an issue of blood. That was the first sign of my crisis...I started bleeding and called the doctor on the same day. This unnamed woman in Mark 5 bled for twelve years with no answers. That would feel like an eternity!

Your story is most likely different because your crisis is most likely different. That's why I like how the KJV records this particular verse, "a woman which had an issue of blood." If you just remove those last two words the verse reads like this:

"*a woman which had an issue.*"

Perhaps you fit that category: you have an issue, a crisis. This woman did. Her crisis, her issue, is named, even though she isn't. Her story has purpose because she shows us how to understand our crises and to have power over them.

Let's move on with her story. Mark 5:26 (NIV), "*She had suffered a great deal under the care of many doctors and had spent all she had, yet instead of getting better she grew worse.*"

- She suffered a great deal
- Went to numerous doctors
- She's spent all she had, therefore, she's broke
- She got worse instead of better
- This went on for 12 years

This isn't mentioned in the text, but history teaches us that she would have been considered an outcast in society; she would not have been allowed to live with her family. Nor would she have been allowed to associate with her friends or be a part of her community. As long as a woman was bleeding, no matter the reason, she was considered unclean. Anything she touched was considered unclean, which meant no one else could use whatever she had come in contact with until it was purified, made clean, restored in a ceremonial cleansing.

However, since she had been bleeding for 12 years, she would be an outcast, living in an area reserved for her and others who couldn't associate with the *clean* people. She wasn't allowed to draw water from the community well when others were; she would have to go at inconvenient times, when no one else was there.

She could only speak with other people who were also ostracized. This would pose all kinds of other issues. How do people in crisis encourage others in crisis? How does a broken person offer help to another broken person?

This woman was *subject* to her issue. That means her crisis dominated her, it controlled her.

Mark 5:27 *"When she heard about Jesus, she came up behind Him..."*

This frustrated, broken, at her wits end, sick and tired, lonely, empty, discouraged woman in a crisis makes a decision out of desperation and it proves to be the best decision she will ever make!

She allows her crisis to lead her straight to the Christ.

Before we go on, we must back up. Why? Well, because there is a significant event going on in the background of this unnamed woman's crisis.

And she is completely unaware of it.

Mark 5:21-24 [21]*"When Jesus had again crossed over by boat to the other side of the lake, a large crowd gathered around him while he was by the lake.* [22]*Then one of the synagogue rulers, named Jairus, came there. Seeing Jesus, he fell at his feet* [23]*and pleaded earnestly with him, "My little daughter is dying. Please come and put your hands on her so that she will be healed and live."* ²⁴*So Jesus went with him. A large crowd followed and pressed around him."*

Jesus had barely gotten out of the boat and a crowd gathers around Him. Mark describes this crowd as a large crowd. Understanding this passage in the Greek language makes for a very interesting description of this crowd. There are certain words in other languages that when translated to English miss the full, deep intent of their meaning. That's another reason why I love to see what some words translate back to in their original language when studying the Bible.

Take for instance, the word *crowd* in verses 21 and 24. It's the same word in each verse, even in the Greek, and it simply means *a casual collection of common people*. At the end of verse 24 it says that this casual collection of common people *pressed* Him (Jesus). The KJV uses an interesting word here: thronged. *"Much people followed Him and thronged Him."* Thronged means to choke, strangle, drown. When the KJV says, "Much people followed Him and thronged Him," literally, what this means is a shoulder-to-shoulder mass of people; a sea of people were pressing in on every side of Jesus as He was on the move.

"And a certain woman who had an issue was there..."

In this choking, massive sea of people there is a woman. With an issue. In this common collection of people, seemingly drowning to see Jesus, to be near Jesus, there is a woman in crisis. And she comes up behind Jesus.

But someone has beaten her to Him. A lot of someones have beaten her to Jesus' side. They're literally jammed packed like sardines to see Jesus. At the moment there is one man who believes he has Jesus' complete attention. Jairus. We see him mentioned in verse 22.

²² *"Then one of the synagogue rulers, named Jairus, came there. Seeing Jesus, he fell at his feet."*

He, too, is a real person, with a real crisis in this pressing, thronging, choking sea of common, ordinary people. Except in that day he would not be considered so ordinary. The verse refers to Jairus as a synagogue ruler. He had an important, prestigious position. He was a ruler. In the synagogue. He had enormous responsibility and authority, a position of honor; he would have been extremely respected. He was a significant leader. This man would be a man of influence, a judge-like authority, he would have been sought after in order to have answers for any difficult situation that came his way. And yet, this ruler who is familiar to maintaining order suddenly finds his life out of order and in need of help. Jairus is in a crisis.

Even though Jairus is in a crisis, he does the same thing our unnamed friend does. He allows his crisis to lead him straight to the Christ.

Jairus falls at the feet of Jesus and pleads earnestly for this intensely popular man, Jesus, who is currently being thronged, pressed, choked by a sea of people, to come to his house and put His hands on his daughter, who is sick and dying. His desire is for his daughter to be healed.

When this woman, this gutsy, bold, live-life-on-the-edge-without-falling-to-pieces kind of woman comes up behind Jesus in this crowd...this choking, massive sea of people she is completely unaware that anyone else is desperately in need of whatever this Jesus has to offer. She is only focused on her crisis. Who can blame her? She is sick and tired, frustrated, lonely, fed-up, discouraged, and desperate. After all, she's been in her crisis for twelve years.

Here is some good news for her and for Jairus: there is plenty of Jesus to go around.

I am reminded of the more-than-enoughness of Jesus each time I receive communion. I love when the bread and the juice are offered as a means of grace to remember what Jesus did on the cross. I'm reminded of His suffering and death so that anyone who calls on His Name will be saved from the penalty of their sins and saved to a lasting, eternal relationship with God. When the bread is offered in already broken pieces I usually take a few pieces. When the loaf is whole and I get to rip a piece of bread off the loaf, I take a chunk of bread. I want a big piece of Jesus.

It is crucial for this woman, for Jairus, and for anyone facing a crisis to understand two things:

- Jairus, our unnamed friend, you, and I have a greater need than for Jesus to heal our crisis or to make our issues disappear.
- There is always someone paying attention to you in your crisis.

First of all, we all have the same basic need: to be saved from our sin. We need a Savior. We need Jesus, who is the Savior. Now Jairus and this unnamed woman haven't heard of the cross because Jesus hasn't hung on the cross yet. He's on His way, though. In a couple of years He'll be crucified and then Jairus and this woman will be able to know Jesus not only as the Miracle Maker, but as their personal Lord and Savior, Jesus Christ.

Jairus and the unnamed woman lived on *that side of the cross.* We live on, what many refer to as, *this side of the cross.* He's been crucified and He has already died. He's been laid in the tomb and He already rose from the dead!

John 3:16 says He did this because God loved the world so much that He provided the plan. His beloved Son would leave heaven, come to earth as a Baby (to be God with skin on) and would one day die on a cross and rise from the dead. Since then all of humanity would have the opportunity to believe in Jesus as the Son of God, accept God's free gift of salvation, and live with God the Father, God the Son, and God the Holy Spirit, forever!

That's our greatest need: we have need of a Savior; One Who saves us from our sins. Jesus did not come to meet our expectations; He came to meet our need. You may have the expectation of Jesus to make your crisis, your issues go away. And He's certainly able to do it. But your need of a Savior trumps your need to be issue-less.

Jesus is on the way to Jairus' house. He doesn't go because Jairus asked. Jesus went to Jairus' house because He was God's Son on assignment from God. Being God with skin on made Jesus an agent of God's grace. God has compassion on Jairus. God shows mercy. God accepts Jairus and loves Jairus right where he's at; BUT He loves Jairus too much to leave him there. God loves Jairus, because God is love and all God does begins right from that place: love.

Not only do people in crisis share the same basic need, they also have people paying attention to their crisis. Better said, there's always a crowd watching your crisis.

There's always an audience, not always a large, pressing, thronging massive sea of people; sometimes the audience is quite small. Regardless, there will always be at least one other person paying attention to your crisis; watching you in your crisis. Someone may be waiting for you to fall to pieces. Someone may be gazing at the opportunity to catch you reacting to your crisis. What will you let them see? Will they see someone falling to pieces or will *Someone* shine bigger and brighter than your crisis?

God made me very aware of this fact in my crisis. My first audience was the people I lived with - my husband and my four children. As you read my son's English assignment in chapter 6, you saw that he was a captive audience. The crowd watching me wasn't as great as the sea of people pressing around Jesus, but it was a crowd: extended family, friends, neighbors, people in the community, doctors, nurses, church family, the ladies in the Bible Study I taught, other fans sitting around me at the high school basketball and baseball games, women attending the events I was asked to speak at, those who read my public posts on carepages.com, friends on

Facebook, strangers I would sit next to in a restaurant or walk down the same aisle in a grocery store with; the list goes on. The audience is great when we pay attention to it.

I doubt the unnamed woman in Mark 5 was paying attention to all the people paying attention to her.

Some might read Mark 5:28, "*...she thought, 'if I just touch His clothes, I will be healed...*'" and think that the woman's faith is actually small.

Folks, let's not look at the size of the faith. Faith is a lot like being pregnant. A pregnant lady isn't a little pregnant; she either is or she isn't. She may not show that she's pregnant, but it doesn't mean she isn't. Faith works in the same way. You either have it or you don't.

Jesus Himself said that if you have faith of a mustard seed you'll be able to move mountains. (Matthew 17:20). This woman who was in a crisis for twelve years has somehow heard of this Jesus and she musters up enough faith, even if her mustering faith was the size of a mustard seed it was enough. Why? Because it's not about how much faith one has, it's about the direction of the faith.

Faith requires an object. As a Christian, a believer, if you tell someone "just have faith" then you're leaving out the best part of that phrase. Make sure you put the object of the faith in the phrase "have faith *in Jesus.*" Faith without Jesus is empty and will fail. Faith, for a believer in Jesus, must be rooted in Jesus, placed in Jesus, and rely on Jesus.

When you're in a crisis the direction of your faith makes all the difference. Jairus had his faith in Jesus. When this woman approached Jesus from behind and thought *oh, if I just touched His clothes, then I'll be healed* she, too, had her faith and her focus on Jesus. She was so focused on Jesus, convinced of His healing power that all she needed was to touch Him. She just wanted to go unnoticed and to touch the hem of His garment. The word *touch* means *to fasten to* or *adhere to.*

If I could just cling to the cloak of the Christ.

This woman's faith in Jesus propelled her to want to fasten her fingers to the fringe.

Her faith held zero power. The object of her faith, Jesus, He holds all the power! The Christ in the middle of your crisis, He holds all the power for your crisis, as well. Even in small doses, He's enough.

Mark 5:29 *"Immediately her bleeding stopped..."*

How fast? How quickly? Immediately. That's pretty fast. That's quick. Does it get any faster than immediately? *Immediately her bleeding stopped.* One moment she's bleeding and BAM!!! Not anymore. Folks...that should cause you to be jumping up and down right now, or letting out a huge, "Hallelujah!" That is incredible! That is amazing! That is miraculous! That is astounding! That is awesome! That is unbelievable!

This is the power in a crisis.

This is Jesus!

And yet it gets better. What?!?! How can that miracle get any better?

Mark 5:29 *"...she felt in her body that she was freed from her suffering."*

Once again our Lord blows me away. And it's a part of our Lord that we can miss if we're not careful, especially while in a crisis. This is a must. This is essential. This is crucial to keep us from falling to pieces in our crisis.

SHE WAS HEALED, YES, BUT EVEN BETTER THAN THAT... SHE WAS *FREED*!

In this journey called life, those who belong to Jesus and who are in crisis need to remember that it is not enough to be crisis-less. There are times when we only pray for God *to make the crisis go away.* Yes, Jesus can heal you. Yes, Jesus can make any crisis go away. Yes, He can fix a financial problem, get you a job, bring home your wayward child, lead you to the right man or woman, heal your cancer; He's God. He's the Mighty Miracle Maker. He can do it because nothing is impossible with God. However, until you see that He is far more interested in *FREE*ing you, than healing you, you'll be stuck; you'll be incomplete.

There are people, perhaps even you, who indeed have been healed, have had Jesus perform a miracle in your life and yet you're still in bondage, stuck. Like this woman in Mark 5, you don't *need* to be healed in order to be freed. This woman could have crawled away, still bleeding, but because she had an encounter with Jesus, because He freed her, she could still have been made whole.

Her wholeness was not dependent on her healing.

However, for her, Jesus freed her *AND* He healed her.

Mark 5:30 "*At once, Jesus realized that power had gone out from Him. He turned around in the crowd and asked, 'Who touched my clothes?'*"

People are elbow to elbow, shoulder to shoulder. This crowd has been described as a choking sea of people. People are everywhere. And Jesus asks who touched His clothes? Yes, He asks. Why? Because He's curious? Because He's confused? Because He didn't know the answer? Nope. He asks for two reasons:

- He wants her wholeness to be made complete
- He knows someone in the audience is paying attention

Mark 5:33 "*Then the woman, knowing what had happened to her, came and fell at his feet and, trembling with fear, told him the whole truth.*"

Her encounter with Jesus Christ required a response. How did she respond?

She fell at His feet. She trembled with fear and told Him the whole truth. The *whole* truth. And nothing but the truth. So God did help her!

Did you know that Jesus can handle the truth? He can handle your scared, trembling emotions. You're actually better off laying those emotions at His feet than you would be keeping them inside. She had a lot bottled up inside of her: 12 years of doubt, 12 years of fear, 12 years of frustrations, 12 years of loneliness, 12 years going broke, 12 years of anger, and she laid it all at His feet. And she instantly knew freedom; a freedom that only Jesus offers and brings to a heart.

Mark 5:35 *"While Jesus was still speaking, some men came from the house of Jairus, the synagogue ruler. 'Your daughter is dead,' they said. "Why bother the teacher anymore?"*

Jairus was in the audience. Jairus was paying attention to this unnamed woman in her crisis. He had a front and center view of this whole event as it unfolded. Jairus began paying close attention as soon as Jesus stopped, turned around, and inquired of who touched His clothes. When this terrified woman turns around and falls at Jesus' feet and begins telling her story, Jairus was listening; he's paying attention; very close attention. He watched as Jesus immediately realized that power had gone out of Him. He watched as Jesus asked who touched His clothes. He watched. Closely.

Jesus reacted to the power that had gone out of Him and onto and into her.

This power that discharged from God's Son is the power that can only come from God. It's called *dunamis*. That's the Greek word used in English to mean power. Dunamis: God's strong, healing, and miraculous power. The word dynamite derives from dunamis. God's explosive, strong, healing, miraculous power discharged from Jesus and into her. And Jesus knew it; He felt it. And Jairus is paying attention.

Jairus heard the woman tell Jesus the whole truth. He heard Jesus tell this woman to "go in peace and be freed." (Mark 5:34) Scripture says that while Jesus was still speaking to the woman

Jairus received earth-shattering, awful, horrible, devastating news that began another crisis inside of him.

How in the world can this man not fall to pieces in this particular crisis? The voice of despair, the voice of destruction, the voice of devastation has spoken to Jairus.

Just because the voice of despair, destruction, and devastation speaks doesn't mean it has to have your full and complete attention. Jesus was still speaking to the woman, but He's God and He also had His focus in Jairus' direction.

Mark 5:36 "*Ignoring what they said, Jesus told the synagogue ruler, "Don't be afraid; just believe."*

Jesus turns to Jairus and I can just imagine Him getting in Jairus' face, maybe even hands on the sides of his head, holding Jairus' gaze. "Ignoring what they said..." *Jairus, stop listening to the outside voices; Jairus, focus right here; you came to me when you thought your daughter was only sick...your circumstances do not change who I am.*

Jesus' words were the same to me when I was in my crisis. His words have power.

Power in your crisis comes from listening to the voice of One. The voice of Truth. The voice, the hands, the touch, the eyes of Jesus; they all have the same explosive power. Dunamis! This power is a never-ending, constant, steady, source that is available in mass quantities from God.

His power can heal. His power does heal. His power can bring freedom. His power does bring freedom. His power can make you whole. His power *does* make you whole. His power can penetrate through the loud voice of doubt and despair.

"Don't be afraid; just believe."

Literally that means, "Don't bolt, trust my power."

Jairus, stick with Me, trust Me, trust My power. Trust *My* power, *My* dunamis, the same power you just saw explode in that woman's life. Focus on that, on Me. I am the power in your crisis. It's My power, and My power alone, that will help you to not fall to pieces in this crisis. Make Me and My power your focus, I know the crisis is here, I know the crisis is hard, I know the crisis seems unbearable. I know your inclination is to doubt, to bolt, to be afraid, to be angry, to give up, to waver, to feel as if you're about to lose all control; I know. Just hang on to Me. Trust in Me. Trust My power.

If you want to know the rest of Jairus' story, you'll have to finish Mark 5 for yourself. Focus on the power of Christ in the midst of the crisis. His power, dunamis, is what causes us to not fall to pieces in our crises.

The whole time I was in my crisis I never once prayed for physical healing. I never once prayed for the cancer to go away. I knew hundreds of other people were praying for me and I was really good with that. I believe in the power of prayer. Since God had shown me that this was His assignment for me, that He had allowed the crisis, the cancer, in my life, I didn't want to miss any of the lessons He had for me to learn. I wanted to be focused on Him. Like Jairus, I felt Jesus was holding my gaze, pleading with me to look into His eyes, encouraging me to ignore all other voices, and to trust in His power alone; that same explosive power that freed an unnamed woman and made her whole and caused a man not to fall to pieces in his crisis.

CHAPTER 8

Peace vs. Piece in the Crisis

Know Jesus? Know peace.
No Jesus? No peace.

Perhaps you're familiar with that phrase.

It's pretty plain and simple.

When Humpty Dumpty fell off that wall, he fell to pieces. He was a broken mess. So broken in fact, that no one could put him back together again.

I was determined in my crisis that I would not fall to pieces. The only way that was going to happen was if the Prince of Peace was invited into my crisis to rule over my pieces. When faced with a crisis we all have the same options:

- Lean on the Prince of Peace
- Fall to pieces

I choose option #1.

My dad is a special man to me. He's been one of the greatest examples of what it means to be a follower of Christ. He's loved my mom and been committed to her and their marriage since 1962.

He has been a decent provider, having a few different careers over the years. Not because he couldn't hold one down for longer than a few years, not because he got antsy, not for any other reason than God called him out of one career so He, God, could use my dad as a pastor.

Being from the suburbs of the Motor City, Detroit, dad got a job at Ford Motor Company at the age of 18. He worked 30 years there and retired. Retired at 48. After that retirement he worked an hourly position at a local business, just to keep busy. At the age of 55 my dad became a full time pastor. This required that he move his family, my mom and my younger sister, to a different community, put a "for sale" sign in the yard of the house they had lived in for 26 years, and begin a journey only God could orchestrate for a man at his age and station in life.

For my entire life I have witnessed my dad, Allen Schweizer, follow Jesus. And he has been a passionate follower; a dedicated disciple. He speaks of being a once painfully shy guy, with a shattered self-image problem; a horrible identity crisis. But I only know the man who has always taken a stand for the Gospel of Jesus, a man never timid to show who he lived for, a man who obediently lives each and every day for His Savior. A man whose relationship with Jesus is "current and up-to-date," a phrase he is known to challenge others with at times.

The passion my dad has is, at times, an internal passion; most of the time it's an external expression, an outward display of the passionate love he has for his Lord. As a young girl I was embarrassed by this display. I now respect, love, admire, and desire the zeal he exhibits.

As I was growing up we attended a church that worshiped in the morning service with a more traditional style. Those roots have been a blessing for me, roots I highly treasure. Each Sunday the congregation would raise their voices together, in unison, to recite a creed, an authoritative statement that describes beliefs.

My dad took that word 'authoritative' to heart. When my dad recited a particular creed, he meant what he said; he took those words seriously.

Anyone in the sanctuary knew that Allen Schweizer believed and lived what he was reciting. Though boisterous, and often demonstrative, it never distracted from the direction the words coming off his lips were headed. The words of the creed, though rote, began in his heart, traveled to his brain, flew off his tongue, reflected on his face, and attached to the heart and throne of God in an act of worship.

Dad was the song leader, now we call them worship leaders, for years during the evening worship service. The Sunday evening worship services were more contemporary. We used hymnals, but not the same ones as Sunday mornings; they were more peppy and lively hymns. At times, the hymnals were exchanged for chorus books. We would sing a few songs in a row, standing the whole time. Some would clap hands or raise their arms in praise; "Hallelujahs" and "Amens" were shouted.

Dad was the loudest voice heard; not for show, he was good and talented, but he made sure the talent God gave him was used for God's glory at all times. He was often demonstrative in his song leading. If he felt led by God's Spirit to hold out a note, we all held out that note, as an act of praise to God.

During these Sunday evening worship experiences people were given opportunities to share testimonies; a current God-sighting in their life. They would pop up like popcorn to stand and share where God had worked in their life that past week. A Biblical message, a sermon, was given that challenged the listeners to go deeper in their relationship with Jesus. And every Sunday evening, and often in the mornings, an altar call was given; an invitation to come to the altar and pray.

As a little girl I would watch the same people who gave testimonies come forward and pray on their knees about all kinds of matters. Not all testified, not all went to the altar, but my dad was one who did both. Not all the time. But enough to make an impact on me. I love to hear the stories of how the wood on the rails would need to be refinished due to the snot and the tears that were shed at the altar.

Even though my dad sang loud, prayed loud, and spoke a creed loud, I never once heard him raise his voice in anger toward my mom. I've never heard him say a cuss word. Oh, he would get angry at times, but he never used the pitch or depth of his voice as a way to express that anger. He would be controlled as he communicated during those difficult times when anger was present.

Peace, never pieces, for my dad.

My dad would begin each day in prayer. Before heading to his office at Ford Motor Company he would be on his knees in a quiet spot of our house. I would love to hear him say my name as he prayed. A couple of times I would stick my ear to the door and wait to hear my name fall off his lips in prayer to our Lord. Significant? Absolutely. It's called integrity.

My dad has lived a life of integrity and I respect and love him for it. I praise God for this example in my life. I praise God that my dad has been an agent of peace, for me. My dad has been one of the best role models of how to trust in the Prince of Peace as opposed to falling to pieces in a crisis.

My dad is wise and I can trust his advice. My dad is smart and I can trust his knowledge. My dad is committed to His Savior and I can trust his example.

My dad has often referenced particular statements during my lifetime. These mantras, repeated phrases, are obvious truths to my dad that he chooses to live by. These repetitions are like glue and stuck to his integrity; some have been evident for years. And he is not shy to share them or challenge others with them. For instance, for as long as I can remember my dad will refer to a hardship, a trial, an adversity, a difficulty, or a crisis as a *Praise-the-Lord-situation*.

- The car breaks? It's a *Praise-the-Lord-situation.*
- The chicken pox invaded our home? It's a *Praise-the-Lord-situation.*
- In band I didn't get first-chair flute player? It was a *Praise-the-Lord-situation.*
- Grandpa is in a serious car accident? It's a *Praise-the-Lord-situation.*

He wouldn't say that to trivialize the difficulty or ignore the emotions involved. He said it to make sure that he and others listening knew where his focus was. The broken car wasn't a good thing, it was a frustration. It would cost extra money to be fixed and schedules would get disrupted causing people to be inconvenienced. Though all inconveniences are true, he would deal with each circumstance connected to the trial and make sure the first thing to recognize was that not one tragedy, not one adversity, not one hardship, not one crisis would ever get more attention than His Lord would get. Always peace, never pieces.

I remember the evening I told my parents their daughter had cancer; that I had cancer. Mom and Dad were already planning to come over that night, though they had no clue this crisis was now part of our family. Since Kevin and I had planned on spending that weekend away, my parents were going to have some Troy-time. They were coming to our house to pick Troy up for the weekend. (At 15, a freshman in high school, he still loved going to his grandparent's house for visits.) I decided to wait to tell them of the diagnosis when we were face-to-face.

They weren't in the house very long when I told them I had something I needed to share with them. My mom began to cry, not out of weakness, but out of a mother's intuition. I didn't allow any time to be suspended in that space. I just came right out and told my parents the truth.

"Mom, Dad, I have cancer. It's not good."

Mom immediately came over to the couch I was sitting on and wrapped her mother arms around me and held me as we both cried. At 45 years of age, that still felt right, safe, and good.

My dad is a processor. I could tell he was mulling this news over in his head. But it didn't take very long for him to bring his fatherly, daddy self over to his daughter, look her square in the eye and say, "Honey, this is certainly a *Praise-the-Lord-situation*. I love you. We'll pray for you. We trust you to God." And then I got the hug.

My dad spoke the same truth into me he had lived out for years. He just found out his daughter had a high risk, aggressive form of cancer, that she would need surgery, chemotherapy, and radiation and his words brought comfort and peace to me and my newly named crisis.

My parents have both been fantastic supports throughout my crisis.

Mom is a true servant, a huge help. She loves to clean, cook, iron, do laundry, wash windows, vacuum, dust, and run errands. (Based on all that, it's comical to me that we even share DNA.) She has been a blessing and brought peace to my crisis in so many ways...my Manna Momma, for sure!

Both mom and dad showed up at a couple of my chemo treatments. They came to my home and stayed for days at a time so mom could lend her servant-like help with all the household responsibilities. They've prayed, they've asked many, many other people to pray for me and my family. Peace, not pieces, from my parents.

The community we lived in at that time sponsored an annual event to raise funds and awareness for cancer research in places around the world. It's a weekend-long event where teams of people gather around a track or make-shift track to continually have representatives walk in memory of those who have fought and in honor of those who are fighting cancer. One particular lap around the track is for survivors of cancer. It's called the survivor lap. There could be hundreds of people walking at the same time who all have one thing in common. They share the same crisis.

After the lap there's commonly a ceremony for survivors of cancer with a survivor invited to share their story of hope. In 2010 I was the one invited to share my crisis story. Any time I have the opportunity to share my story, I take it. I want to honor God by sharing the hope I have in Jesus, crisis or no crisis. He is worth sharing about! True hope comes from the same place true peace comes from: the Prince of Peace, Jesus Christ! He is the only One capable and able to scoop up any and all pieces in a crisis and make His peace reign.

My dad had a wise word for me the day I shared my story of hope at the Survivor Ceremony. After the survivor walks his/her lap then their care givers are encouraged to walk the next lap with them. My husband, my four children and I held hands and walked in a long line around the track. My parents and my sisters walked right behind us. As the lap came to an end my dad came up to my side and said, "Ellen, as I read the Bible I don't notice the word survivor in there, but I do see victor."

I loved that. I respect the term, survivor, made popular by a non-profit organization and I proudly wear the tee-shirts I have from them. There is absolutely nothing wrong with anyone referring to themselves as a survivor: a person who continues to function or prosper in spite of opposition, hardship, or setbacks.

But I needed to be reminded of a very important truth and God used my dad as His mouthpiece to speak that truth into me:

Survivor or Victor? *Survive-or* Victor?

I choose victor:

A person who has overcome or defeated an adversary; a conqueror.

A winner in any struggle or contest.

Those people who are in relationship with Jesus through the cross are always victors. This victory has nothing to do with the crisis and everything to do with Jesus! It's because we have victory in Jesus! He overcame death, He conquered the grave therefore, as heirs to all Jesus did, and all Jesus is, and all Jesus has; *we are victors*!

I can only survive because I'm a victor!
That brings peace to the pieces of my crisis.

Thanks, Dad!

**mom, me, dad; the only time he's ever worn a
bandana...just for his victorious daughter**

In December 2009, the night before my surgery, I had a test of where my focus, my attention, would be in my crisis.
Would I fall to pieces or lean on the Prince of Peace?
It was my choice.

My son Eric was a junior in high school. It was the month the varsity basketball team began their season. On this night before my surgery we received a phone call that Eric needed us at the gym where his team was gathered for practice. Since I was home preparing for my upcoming surgery scheduled for early the next day Kevin went to the gym. What did he find? He found our son in the midst of his own crisis.

Our son, captain of the team; the excited, hard working, focused, talented, athlete had badly sprained his ankle. Not just a tweak or a twist of the ankle, rather, one of the worst types of sprains an athlete can suffer. This momma had her heart broke for her son. This momma found herself with more pieces falling in her life.

I was at home, in my bedroom, attempting to rest. I was focused on my crisis; the recent diagnosis, surgery the next day, not to mention the promised, pending treatments and all the unknowns due to this recent crisis that erupted in my life. I was praying for a number of things.

As soon as word came to me that Eric was being taken to the hospital due to a basketball injury my prayer focus changed. My emotional space increased so that my son's crisis could have room in the already crowded area of my life. Like a snap of the fingers, my mind was no longer focused on me, but on my son who was hurting, who was experiencing his own crisis.

It took weeks for my 3-point shooter son to join his team that season and participate fully in their games. As I was home convalescing, healing from the surgery, and preparing for my upcoming chemo treatments, Eric was on crutches, waiting for his ankle to slowly heal. As a mom it was so difficult to watch my son deal with his crisis. Yet, his crisis taught me lessons.

God showed me that though I was personally in a crisis that I was to not ignore the fact that others around me could very well be in their own crisis and I needed to think of them, pray for them, and pay attention to them. My son didn't need a mom who was falling to pieces, he needed a mom who was centered, focused, and leaning on the everlasting arms of the Prince of Peace.

When we named our four eldest children we didn't have a set formula we applied. I looked in the ever popular baby name book we had purchased when I was pregnant with Christine, narrowed our options down to about 10 choices and then we practiced their first names. How does one practice a name?

Well, I would practice saying the name in different settings: "Eric, mommy loves you," said very sweetly. "Go pick up your toys, Eric," spoken with authority. I would practice opening the front door of the house, pretending he was down the street playing with future friends, and I would yell, "Eric, time for dinner!!" Then there was my personal favorite: "Eric!" said with a finality that meant *you-better-stop-fighting-with-your-brother-right-now-buddy-and-apologize.* Yup, I was practiced and ready to name him. It worked. I loved saying it sweetly, I liked speaking it with authority, and I even appreciated the sound of it with the mother-yell.

Kevin, on the other hand, practiced this way: he would pretend he was in a gym. The basketball game was coming to an end, the score was tied, and his son was shooting the final basket of the game, a free throw shot. And he would practice-chant, "Errric, Errric, Errric!" Yup, that worked, too.

We gave him the name Eric, which means *always ruler.* That's appropriate for this natural-born-leader son of ours. He lives up to that meaning with integrity. Kevin and I could take credit for naming our son Eric Allen, but we have seen over the years that God was involved in naming him.

Eric Allen. It gives me great joy to know one of my children bears the name, Allen, after my dad. I pray Eric will not only bear the name but also wear his name, Allen, like his grandpa who is an agent of peace to others, a man who has chosen to never fall to pieces in a crisis, a man who loves Jesus Christ with his whole heart, and is completely sold out for the cause of Christ. A man, who though his name means *always ruler,* will choose to *always be ruled* by the Prince of Peace, never falling to pieces in any crisis, just like his grandpa, my dad.

Know Jesus? Know peace.
No Jesus? No peace.

CHAPTER 9

Possibility & Promise after the Crisis

July 2010 was a great time for me and Kevin. We felt like life was starting to settle into a 'new normal' of sorts for us. Treatments were past. Another CT scan, x-rays, and a check up with the gynecologic oncologist showed no recurrence of the cancer. I was told I should never refer to myself as cancer free; the correct way to communicate my status is to say *the cancer has not recurred.* July brought this good news to us. At the very end of that same month we were at a very special place.

In 1997 my family was introduced to a Christian Camping Ministry called Bay Shore Camp. Bay Shore holds a special place in each of our hearts. Our kids have been to many of the age-appropriate weekly summer camps as well as some themed camps (i.e. sports camps, music camps.) Kevin and I have attended retreats; we've each served on the board of directors; we've been in charge of a children's camp. I've directed musicals for the music camps. I've spoken at various women's events/retreats. We have been blessed by the ministry of this special place called Bay Shore Camp in Sebewaing, MI.

It wasn't until our oldest, Christine, wrote a paper in college where she mentioned her favorite place on earth was Bay Shore Camp that Kevin and I realized we hadn't considered her particular perspective. Since Christine had lived in seven different houses prior to leaving for college she sees Bay Shore Camp as the one constant place in her life. She mentioned in the paper that life-changing/life-altering decisions were made at Bay Shore Camp. She said that God has spoken to her heart in special ways at Bay Shore. She's experienced possibility and promise at this special place. We all have experienced possibility and promise at Bay Shore Camp.

Since 1997 it is at this place where our family has attended Family Camp each summer. Even as our older children have graduated from high school, attended college, and gotten settled on their career paths they still attempt to clear their busy summer schedules so we can be at this one place together as a family, worshiping our Lord, and spending quality time as a family. We attend daily Bible studies and evening worship experiences. Not only is my mother's heart full as we attempt to fill an entire row in the old, wooden, open tabernacle, but I especially love that for one whole week I have the opportunity to sit next to my preacher husband where he's not preaching. (Don't get me wrong, I love hearing my husband preach; I have been stretched in my faith, grown in my love of my Savior, challenged by the Word of God, and taught new insights from the Bible through Kevin's preaching.) But...I love sitting next to my man as we've heard good, solid, and challenging preaching during family camp each summer.

In July 2010, while we were sitting in the very tabernacle where we had sat for 13 summers in a row, Kevin and I heard God speak clearly and concisely into our 'new normal.' It was a hot night. The preacher was preaching. We had our pens ready to write notes in the margins of the open Bibles sitting on our laps. Kevin's arm was draped across my shoulders on the old wooden pew. He was comfortably slouched, one leg crossed over and resting on the other knee in his ready-to-listen-and-pay-close-attention mode. I was nestled in close to him. We were open to God's message. And boy did He have a message for the Harbin's!

I could not tell you what the preacher was preaching on that particular hot July night. Yet, God still had a message for us. During the sermon God spoke to Kevin and I. Same God. Same message. And it was the same message He had spoken to us months earlier, prior to my crisis. The message?

"Kevin and Ellen, you are still on My same assignment," God said, "You are to adopt."

WHAT?!?!?! Did I just hear that right? In the middle of the sermon, while the preacher is preaching God spoke into my heart. What I didn't know was at that exact moment God was speaking the same message into Kevin's heart.

I sat in amazement as I pondered these words of possibility that were once words of promise; a possibility that got run over; a promise that appeared broken due to a crisis that got in the way. Yet, did it really? Did a crisis mess up a promise? Did a crisis squelch a possibility?

Not at all.

Kevin and I questioned and wondered how we had misinterpreted God's call on our life to adopt. *How did we get it so wrong? How was the idea of adopting children something that seemed so right? Every door had been flung open wide as we approached adoption. Every step along the way appeared to be God-made, God-led, and God-approved.* It was as if we were punched in the gut, blindsided by our crisis.

But we were a couple who refused to fall to pieces in our crisis. We refused to allow our crisis to dictate God's potential possibility and promise to us. We knew that even though cancer had come uninvited into our lives that we would wait on God. We needed to continue trusting in His omniscience, His all-knowing power, to see what His plans were for our family. We were open to His leading; we only desired to be led by Him. Even if that meant being led away from a plan we anticipated, a plan we had once welcomed.

When Kevin and I elbowed each other during the sermon that hot night in July and shared the message we had each just received from God individually, we were elated, overjoyed! The adoption option was never cancelled; it was just derailed, disrupted for a time. It had been maneuvered; it had been in Omniscient's hand the whole time.

In August, 2010 I called Pam, our case worker at the Methodist Children's Home Society. I asked her if we could reopen our closed case file. She immediately replied with an "Absolutely!" It would require a few more steps. I would have to have a doctor sign off on my cancer status, stating that as far as they knew the status of my health was stable. We would also need to have some of our home study redone since portions of it are only good for a year.

We once again began communicating with Pam. We picked up where we left off a year earlier, we set up the necessary appointments, filled out the required paperwork, handed in the mandatory physical/ health qualifications, and we waited for Pam to process it all from her end. Then we waited for the state of Michigan to process it from their end.

This process can take a while. This process can take a great deal of time. However, Pam began referring to our particular process as the *Harbin way.* In other words, there's the way most people experience the process and then there's the way we, the Harbin's, experienced things. Some people thought it absolutely crazy (the good kind of crazy) how efficient and quick things seemed to go for us after I had made that phone call to Pam about reopening our case file.

Two weeks after that initial communication with Pam she called us. This call changed our lives forever, *and* changed the lives of two very precious children who now call me "Mommy."

When I saw on the caller ID that it was the agency, I assumed it was Pam. I also assumed the call would have something to do with needing more paperwork or something got lost and needed resubmitting. I couldn't have been more wrong on the second assumption. My first assumption was correct. It was Pam.

And she was excited! She had two children she wanted us to consider adopting; two children who were waiting for a forever family. She told me their names, their ages, and that they were biological siblings, a brother and sister. She went on to explain that she was sending us a package. In the envelope would be two pictures. Included with the pictures would be their non-identifying information. We would see the general information of when and why these precious children went into the foster system.

Adopting children through the foster system means that each child comes with a story. Not a pleasant story, not a feel-good story. They're in the system because for some sad, tragic, heartbreaking, appalling, unfortunate reason their biological parents' rights have been terminated. Children are never *up for adoption* if there's any chance of reunification with their biological parents, mother or father.

Due to the circumstances that lead any child into this system their history is difficult to deal with, their stories are heart wrenching. But in ALL of the children's situations there is one common factor: they are not at fault for being in the foster system! Each child just needs what all children need: a forever family. You see, when a child is in placement, when parent's rights have been terminated, and they need to be adopted, each child shares the same thing: they've had a family and that didn't work. Now they need a forever family.

When choosing to adopt through the foster system it is crucial to become aware of these facts up front. Kevin and I knew these facts. We were committed to bringing children into our family to become a forever family knowing the instability that existed from their pasts. We were also aware that there were hundreds of children waiting to be adopted through the foster system.

When parents are approved for adoption, they are ready to be matched with children in a process known as *search and match*. Case workers on behalf of the children and the adoptive parents explore a variety of ways to complete this step.

Early on in our journey, prior to my crisis, we began praying for Pam's discernment regarding the *search and match* portion of our journey. We felt strongly that God had already hand-picked our children and He would open Pam's eyes to who they were.

When my cancer crisis entered our lives we assumed the adoption was closed. We were so focused on my health, that it never occurred to us that God could use cancer as a way to answer our prayers for adoption.

When I was pregnant with our four older children we chose not to find out what the gender of each baby was. In the late 1980's and early 1990's it was almost unheard of not to return from that first ultrasound appointment with the picture in hand showing proof of the gender when people inquired, "What are you having?" We approached adoption the same way. We didn't have the answer to that question.

When we made the decision to adopt I began writing in two journals. I wrote notes to two children. Not often, just as I felt led. The first few entries in each journal are written to unnamed children. I wrote things like, "I haven't met you, I don't know your name, I don't know your age. I don't know when I will meet you or hold you. I don't know the color of your skin, your eyes, or your hair. And I don't even know your birthday. But what I do know is that I love you. I love you so much. God began growing a special love for you inside of me when He planted the idea of being your mommy into my heart. I may not have given birth to you through my tummy but I definitely have given birth to you in my heart. I am so glad that God chose me to be your forever mommy."

possibility

God chose me to be a mommy. I love being a mom. Our four oldest showed up rather unexpectedly. Kevin and I had plans of being married for five years before we started having children. By our fifth anniversary we had four kids. Our plan didn't happen the way we thought. God has certainly surprised us a great deal in our many years together. Adoption was another one of His surprises for us: a most welcomed surprise!

Pam is one of the greatest blessings in our adoption journey. She had a job to do and she did it well. She was responsible for making sure we were ready to adopt but more importantly that we were right to adopt. She was also responsible to trust her intuition and have her eyes wide open for children who would fit perfectly in our forever family.

Since Kevin and I had trusted that God was hand-picking our children for us we also trusted that He was guiding Pam to know when the right kids came available. Kevin and I had already decided that when Pam called to say she had a match for us, we would take that as God's leading and say "YES."

Pam called. As she gave me the basic information about the children, I exploded inside with a maternal love; this familiar love that, though it came in a different way with my four older children, was still that same, strong, solid, forever love bursting from within, taking root to the bottom of my heart for a child (and in this case two children) that I hadn't even laid my eyes on.

I experienced that same maternal love years earlier as I entered a bathroom with a pregnancy test in hand and exited with that familiar little stick with a plus sign hanging off the end. The power of the plus sign! This phone call from Pam carried the same kind of intensity, though it didn't come on the end of a stick in the form of a plus sign, it was still the same powerful news: I was going to be a mommy... again!

There is a great deal of information and facts that could be entered here. God's hand did many amazing things. On our best day, on Pam's best day (though she's incredible) only God's hand could have maneuvered people, timetables, foster system expectations, paperwork, and that's just naming a few of the things He orchestrated.

One of the biggest ways we saw His hand stretch out and direct this process, where we saw possibility and promise after the crisis, was what Pam told us about the day I called her to ask if we could reopen our file. Weeks later when we were once again well on our way into the adoption process she shared an amazing story with us. She said that the day before I had called her to reopen our case file she had gone to her supervisor with a concern.

As an adoption case manager she was not only assigned families to connect children with, she was also assigned children who needed a forever family. Pam had been assigned a sibling set, a brother and a sister, whose biological parents' rights had already legally been terminated. This boy and girl had been in a foster home for almost a year and were at the point in their personal journey where case workers, case managers, therapists, and social workers felt they needed to be permanently placed in a forever family through adoption.

Pam had a concern. She just knew in her gut that the Harbin family was the right forever family for these two precious treasures, this sibling set, but the Harbin's case file was closed and legally she couldn't call us to inquire about having our file reopened. She was concerned; she didn't know what to do. The possibility seemed impossible.

I called Pam the next day to reopen our file.

As I write these words for this book I am overcome with emotion. Tears pool in my eyes. They spill out. Kevin and I were clueless that Pam had two children and *just knew in her gut* that we were *the* parents for them. Kevin and I were still overwhelmed from the message we received from God that His plan for us was still the same. We were still in utter amazement that though our adoption assignment got deviated a year earlier due to the cancer crisis that intervened, disrupted, and seemingly crashed our plan to pieces. We were amazed that the God of the impossible, who keeps His promises, and who kept me from falling to pieces when the pieces went tumbling down is the same God Who spoke His plan into our life. He reignited the flame of adoption in our hearts and stirred within Pam the knowledge that we were the exact parents chosen for these two children.

That's possibility and promise after the crisis!

As I step back and look at this incredible journey as one big puzzle, I am taken aback, surprised, humbled, amazed, jaw-dropped, excited, giddy, jubilant, about-ready-to-squeal, at the ways my Lord maneuvered His Hand prior to my crisis, during my crisis, and after the crisis.

When Pam shared with us about the concern she had regarding these two children the day before I called, we were set in stone, solid, immovable, no-doubt, couldn't budge us from the fact that these two children were ours. We just knew God had hand-picked them for us. They needed a forever family and He ignited within us a desire to adopt children in their particular circumstance and, well, He smashed those two entities together.

Had my crisis not come at the time it did then these two children would not be in our family. Why? Because they weren't available for adoption at that time. They became available while my crisis was on-going, when I was in the middle of a crisis.

Did she just say she had a crisis so that they could adopt these particular kids?

NO!! She did not just say that.

It's a matter of perspective. As I stand back and take note of the particular pieces of my crisis; before, during, and after the crisis, I can't help but notice that Sovereign God knew exactly what was going on. He called us to adopt. He knew these children would be in need of a forever family. He knew a crisis was going to erupt in my life. He knew cancer was that crisis. He knew our adoption plan would be set aside. He knew surgery, chemo, and radiation were on the horizon. And through it all, He never once sat on His throne, threw His almighty, everlasting arms in the air and exclaimed "Oh no, now what are we gonna do?"

He didn't cause the cancer.
He didn't cause the crisis.
He didn't cause two children to become orphans.

But He has always been aware of it. And He made sure these two children landed in our family. He made sure I became their mommy....forever.

Possibility and promise.

And I wouldn't change a thing regarding my crisis. I never wished or prayed for it to go away when it came roaring into my life. I've never asked, "Why" it came roaring into my life. While I was on His assignment, while cancer was growing in my body, and while doctors were attempting to remove it and prevent it from recurring and causing further havoc in my life two little children were in a crisis of their own.

Two children were experiencing what no child should ever experience; they were removed from what they knew of and called home. Their biological mother had problems bigger than she could handle, problems that ruled her, issues that took over her mind, her actions, and she lost the right to be their mommy; therefore, they became orphans.

That's a fact about my two youngest children's lives. That's a crisis they lived through. It's a crisis that potentially could affect them, a crisis that could teach them not to consider possibility and promise; not to trust in the God of possibility and promise.

It's my responsibility, along with my husband, their daddy, to teach them that they, too, do not have to let their crisis cause them to fall to pieces. The pieces of their early life are awful. Terrible. They're gut-wrenching, unfair, and unwelcomed. They didn't do anything to deserve what happened. We don't focus there. We don't teach our kids that life was unfair to them, that they were handed a raw deal.

We don't teach them that their birth mom was mean, horrible, or crazy...because she wasn't. She gave my children a gift; she gave them life. She chose to give birth to them. And we love her for that. She made awful mistakes, she allowed herself to be carried away, managed, overtaken by her problems, her issues, but that's not a reason to not forgive her or to not love her.

We teach our kids that the best thing they can do is thank God He provided a forever family for them. He created our family. We all arrived in this forever family in different ways, on different days. Daddy was born a Harbin in 1961. Mommy married into the Harbin family in 1988. Christine arrived in October 1989, in Detroit, MI; Andrew arrived in April 1991, in Farmington Hills, MI; Eric arrived in the same place as Andrew but in January 1993; Troy arrived in December 1994 in Lexington, KY; and Jaylen & Sukanya arrived to the Harbin family on 3 unique dates:

November 2, 2010 is MEET-YA DAY
December 18, 2010 is GOTCHA DAY
July 7, 2011 is ADOPTION DAY

forever

family

We explain to Jaylen and Sukanya that if our family decided to go to New York City and daddy chose to walk; mommy flew in an airplane; Christine, Andrew, Eric, and Troy drove; and that they took a train, though we would all arrive at different times, the important thing is that we all had the same destination. Eventually we would all end up in the same place. That's how it worked for us to become a forever family: we all arrived in different modes of transportation, at different dates and times, but we all arrived in our family.

We hadn't even laid eyes on Jaylen and Sukanya (just like when our biological kids were in my tummy) and we still fell in love; we didn't even know their names (just like when our biological kids were in my tummy) and we still claimed them as our own.

Though we said yes to meeting these two precious children we needed to wait for paperwork to come through before we could legally proceed. On November 1, 2010 Pam called and said we could finally meet Jaylen and Sukanya face-to-face.

Possibility and promise after the crisis.

Kevin and I woke up so excited on November 2, 2010. At 2:00 that afternoon we were to meet at a fast food restaurant one hour away from our house but very close to their foster home. On our way to the meeting place (we were running 20 minutes ahead of schedule) Pam called my cell phone. She asked where we were. I told her we were going to be to the destination at about 1:40. She replied, "Oh good, because I have two very excited children with me right now." She went on, "I told them I had a surprise for them and they began smiling and waiting anxiously to hear what it was. I then told them I was going to take them to meet their mommy and daddy and they haven't stopped screaming, yelling, and jumping up and down since. So I wanted to see if we could get going to the restaurant now."

Our hearts swelled. In a few short moments we would look into two sets of dark brown eyes, hold two dark-skinned children in our white, pale-skinned arms. We would fall deeper in love with these children since we had already loved from afar. We had first loved them as an idea and then fell in love knowing they truly existed. We then fell in love with their names and we fell in love with them knowing of their pasts. We fell in love with their faces in a picture and now we would finally love them face-to-face; touching and holding them: our sweet children.

We didn't really know what to expect as we got out of our car in that fast food parking lot. I had a bag full of crayons, coloring books, games, stickers, pencils, paper, and two small picture albums. We wanted to 'do something' with them; just hang out and enjoy these two children; that explains the stuff in the bag. In each photo album was a picture of Kevin, me, Christine, Andrew, Eric, Troy, the cats, our house, and what would become their elementary school. The picture albums went back to their foster home with them. To this day, those picture albums remain a fixture in their bedrooms, as valued possessions, keepsakes that help prove possibility and promise.

As soon as we entered the restaurant two little beautiful, smiling, black children bounded out of their seats and exclaimed, "Mommy! Daddy!" The bond of mother and child was cemented deep inside my heart at that very moment. I immediately became protective of them. I immediately began desiring to meet their needs. I immediately wanted to pull them under my wing, to keep them safe from all harm, to take care of them, to mother them, *forever*!

That day goes down as one of the best days in our married life! Our wedding day and the days we *met* each of our children face-to-face are top contenders. Each day is forever fixed in my mommy memory bank.

Pam referred to the different steps in our adoption process as "the Harbin way" when steps in the process seemed to go faster than normal. Some things just had no explanation for how and when they got accomplished. Most visitations with foster kids who are preparing for permanent placement in an adoption family, take months before the child/children are ready to move in. Visits go in steps, beginning with a couple of hours with a case worker present, to a few hours without the case worker, to a whole day spent at a neutral sight, to perhaps a visit in the home for a few hours, then a whole day at the family's house. It takes a while, based on how well the children adjust, before they're ready for an overnight visit.

Then there's "the Harbin way."

MEET-YA Day was November 2, 2010, a Tuesday. That next weekend, 3 days later, Jaylen and Sukanya came for the whole weekend. And they came every weekend after that, including Thanksgiving when they stayed for five nights and six days. We loved having them home. We dreaded taking them back to their foster home.

Each Sunday as I drove away after dropping them off I cried, my heart was heavy, I just wanted to be their mommy every minute of every day, forever! We spoke on the phone every day, and it was good, but it was nothing compared to having them in our presence, in our very lives, in our very home, to finally move into our forever family; forever.

Possibility and promise after the crisis.

Pam called. I love when Pam calls. This particular phone call was another one of those "the Harbin way" type of circumstances.

Please don't misinterpret this. Don't take this wrong, because "the Harbin way" of doing things does not have anything to do with us, the Harbins. It's just the phrase Pam affectionately used to make sense of something that didn't make sense in a process that usually has a step-by-step way of getting to the end result. Along the way to the desired goal: adopting children, we faced and experienced God's hand moving obstacles, rerouting a 'normal' way. What we knew as God moving mountains, people at the agency referred to as "the Harbin way."

When Pam called, again, we learned God had moved another mountain. Her supervisor recommended that Kevin and I consider getting a foster license so that the children could legally move into our home once and for all. From the beginning our desire was only to adopt, not to become foster parents, but if we could walk through another door so that our children could legally be in our home forever then we would do it. That's what good parents do: they go through hoops for their kids; they leave no stone unturned for their children's particular needs to be met.

The agency noted how well our children adjusted to their forever family. Pam insisted that whatever needed to take place, within the legal bounds, to get our children into our home needed to be considered. Her supervisor considered, and the outcome was that Kevin and I needed to attend another all-day seminar, a consultation, required by our state in order for a foster license to be issued. We had done all the other necessary prerequisites and this one last piece was necessary.

God moved another mountain. The required all-day session we needed *just happened* to be taking place the next Saturday, and we *just happened* to have an open, empty schedule. There is no such thing as *just happened* or *coincidence;* this was all God and His handiwork! We attended the seminar, Pam registered the paperwork, and God moved another mountain.

The filing of the necessary paperwork that would normally take a few weeks longer than ours actually took, *suddenly, just happened,* to *coincidentally,* land on the exact desk of the person in our state's capital who was responsible for pushing the paperwork through so that the license could be legally obtained.

December 18, 2010 Pam called. She began by saying, "How would you like to go pick up your kids, all their belongings, and never have to take them back again?"

Possibility and promise after the crisis!

December 18, 2010 is now called GOTCHA Day. The day we *got ya*. That was an incredible day. I arrived to their foster home a little early, walked to their corner bus stop, and waited for the bus to arrive. That bus couldn't arrive at that corner fast enough for this mommy! As soon as they exited the bus I asked Jaylen and Sukanya if they would like to "come home, forever!!"

Jumping, squealing, excited, energetic, happy, joyful, children rode in the back of the minivan for the next hour. As soon as we pulled into the driveway, we rushed out of the vehicle, ran to the front door, and crossed the threshold of our house. Kevin met us at the front door and together we let our two youngest children know that they were officially moved in forever...they were forever in our home and that would never, ever change! GOTCHA Day, a day of possibility and promise, is a celebrated day in our family.

It took more than 3 months for our official adoption paperwork to go through the necessary channels at the state's capital, so getting that foster license was a piece we are so thankful for in the whole puzzle of this story. Otherwise, gotcha day would have been 3 months later. As far as our kids are concerned, the day they moved in, GOTCHA day, was the day they became Harbins, forever. Any time their old last name would show up on a piece of paper, like at their new school, at the doctor, or on a report card, we would blame the judge.

We figured we'd put blame or responsibility on someone who would make sense in their young brains. We told them the judge is a *very* busy man. We said that as a judge there were so many other people who needed his attention and though we were in line for him to officially and legally say they were a Harbin, we needed to wait our turn. So we waited. Six months.

July 7, 2011 was ADOPTION Day for our family. That was the day he finally had time to sign his name on a piece of paper that legally made their name change, even though they had been Harbin's for six months, now it was legal and official.

Forever is a good word for children who need a family. You see, they had a family at one time but it didn't work out; referring to ourselves as a Forever Family, as encouraged by all the training we had prior to adopting, is a splendid idea. It gives our kids, and others who have been adopted, an understanding. In one word, *forever,* we explain that we are in this for the long haul, we are never changing our minds, nothing they could do or say will ever change their family status; we are a Forever Family, forever.

Has it been easy? No. And neither was giving birth to four children; and raising those children. Parenting is not for cowards. It is not for the faint of heart. We make mistakes. We fail, at times, but we serve a God of possibility and promise and we trust His wisdom in parenting our two youngest just like we trusted His wisdom in parenting the older four. (I could write a book on this topic alone: parenting children adopted through the foster system, adopting children who come from crisis circumstances.)Their needs are unique; each child's particular idiosyncrasies are to not be ignored.

Possibility and promise after the crisis.

Sukanya, the youngest Harbin. Sukanya Rose Harbin. When we received that initial non-identifying information on her we learned that she was significantly behind academically. She was diagnosed and labeled as cognitively impaired. Her social skills and communication skills were limitations that caused her to learn and develop more slowly than a typical child her age. She was diagnosed through the use of standardized tests of intelligence and adaptive behavior. Her diagnosed *disability* was assumed to be genetic, since standardized tests generally can't be manipulated. I am not a professional on this topic; I am not speaking to it in any official capacity. I am simply stating what was told to us, her parents, so we could better understand what we were facing.

Again, Kevin and I already accepted that Jaylen and Sukanya were our children the day Pam called and said, "I have two kids, a sibling set, I'd like for you to consider adopting." As soon as we heard "I have two kids," we were in: we likened it to finding out we were pregnant. We accepted those babies, the children growing in my womb, exactly as they were. We didn't have the choice of giving them back. We desired to have the same perspective with our adopted children. We accepted these two children *as is*.

The day after we met Sukanya on MEET-YA Day, the foster mom received phone calls from the kindergarten teacher, the school social worker, and the principal.

"What happened to Sukanya?"

"Why?"

"Well, something's happened, we can tell; she's talking, writing, socially connecting with other kids, and joining in conversation. What happened?"

"Well, yesterday afternoon she met her mommy and daddy, that's all that's different."

That's *ALL* that's different? Yes. And that was enough.

She met her mommy. She met her daddy. And she was a changed little girl. We can only explain how a little girl who was diagnosed as *cognitively impaired and would perhaps require special education services her whole life* and is now bench-marked and socially and academically on target as God moving a mountain, God giving possibility and promise to a little girl who only knew crisis as a way of life.

We refuse to fall to pieces in a crisis. We desperately loved this little girl before we even knew her name or what she looked like. We pray she never falls to pieces in a crisis but takes the pieces of her early life to the Prince of Peace so He can bring possibility and promise to her pieces. After all, He loves her far more than this mommy could ever love her; and my love goes so deep I can't even find its beginning. It's rooted. It's planted. It's forever!

This daughter of ours is creative. God has given her a wonderful gift. She expresses herself through drawing, sketching, and coloring. She is amazing. She can make anything out of an empty toilet paper roll or a tissue box. We love seeing whatever new creation she makes on a daily basis. At least once a week I get a question similar to this, "Mommy, can I have this empty box so I can make something with it?" It will be exciting to watch as she uses the gifts and talents God has given to her for His glory.

We gave these two children new middle names. It's one of the most amazing and unbelievable experiences a parent has; to name their child. Their birth mom chose their first names and that's been their identity since the day they were born. We felt that needed to remain intact. It was never an option, a consideration, for us to change their first names. But we did give them new middle names. Much like when we're adopted into God's family, Scripture says we have a new name. We take on the name of Jesus, God's Son. We become like Him, we become instant heirs to His throne, God's kingdom; we belong to the family of God.

Jaylen became *Jaylen Joseph Harbin*. Joseph, like the biblical character who, after experiencing his own crisis, said, "What man meant for harm, God used for good." We desire and we pray that our Jaylen Joseph would tuck in tight to God and allow God to use anything in his life, even the crises from his earliest days, to be used for God's glory. We don't want Jaylen to fall to pieces because of the crises in his life. We want him to see possibility and promise after a crisis.

God has moved in our son's life. Jaylen is a gifted pianist. And no one knew it. One Sunday, months after ADOPTION Day, in the fall of 2011, we came home from church and he began playing a song we had sung in church that morning on a toy keyboard. Possibility was seen. Promise began in this area of Jaylen's life. He has been referred to as a piano prodigy.

At the writing of this book he takes private lessons at a local Institute of Performing Arts. Within six months of beginning to play the piano he performed two recitals; his own recitals. He was the only performer. Each piece he played was done by memory. Currently he's training as a classical pianist. We stand back and listen, we watch, in wonderment and awe at how good God is with this young man. Just like his sister, Sukanya Rose, named after the most beautiful flower in the garden and my mother's maiden name, we see God's Hand in each of their lives. We see what forever love can do.

In 2013 while all eight Harbins were home, we had a Birth Certificate Party. Kevin gathered all eight birth certificates and handed them to their rightful owner. Beginning with the eldest person we each stated the name on the certificate, when they were born, and who the parents were. As each Harbin spoke Jaylen and Sukanya watched and listened with careful attention. When it was Jaylen's turn to read his birth certificate he read his name, "Jaylen Joseph Harbin" then he read, "September 7, 2003." Then we asked him to read who his parents were, "Kevin J Harbin, father; Ellen Schweizer Harbin, mother." Suknaya went next, "Sukanya Rose Harbin, February 9, 2005; Kevin J Harbin, father; Ellen Schweizer Harbin, mother."

These two children saw with their own eyes and held in their own hands their birth certificates, each one from different states. On each document Kevin was their father, I was their mother, just like their four older siblings. We celebrated that. We rejoiced as a family, a forever family, that we all had one thing in common, we shared the same last name. We recognized that each child shared the same father and the same mother. Possibility and promise to two children, their older siblings, and their parents.

As I reflect back to that night in the summer of 2008 when Kevin and I didn't like the sound of quiet we heard and our hearts were opened to an idea, an option called adoption, for our family, I am in awe of how our Lord orchestrated this whole journey. One day our son Eric said something to us like, "Momma & Daddy, I am so thankful momma had cancer. I didn't like that you had it, but if you hadn't had cancer then Jaylen and Sukanya wouldn't be in our family. We would have still adopted kids, but not Jaylen and Sukanya and I can't imagine life without them as a part of our family."

That's a perspective we choose to focus on. Again, God didn't give me cancer so we could adopt our children. God allowed a crisis in my life so I could tuck in tighter to Him, so others could potentially see Christ through my crisis, so that His Son, Jesus could have an opportunity to be glorified and uplifted, in my crisis. I have often said that I would go through this crisis all over again if it meant having Jaylen and Sukanya as my children. They are worth every hardship I experienced on this journey, in this crisis.

I see that though a crisis attempted to come in and destroy a plan, an adoption plan, God taught me that just because it appeared to be destroyed, didn't mean it was destroyed. He didn't desire for me to fall to pieces in my crisis. It wasn't my responsibility to ask "why" this crisis came; He didn't want me to fall apart, He didn't want me to try to figure it out. He wanted me to see Him in it; not causing it, but allowing it, for some purpose; for some possibility and some promise to one day show up and blow me away with His goodness.

And I am indeed, blown away, by His protection, His provision, His power, His peace, His possibility, and His promise.

I am blown away by what I learned, what I saw, what I experienced before, during, and after my crisis as a result of refusing to fall to pieces in my crisis.

I pray you are drawn to the Christ. I pray you choose to see the Christ before, during, and after any crisis you may face.

After all, as God's Word says,

"If you fall to pieces in a crisis there wasn't much to you in the first place." Proverbs 24:10

2013, celebrated 25 years of marriage

Concluding Thoughts

By: Kevin Harbin

I have often said, "I went to seminary to train for my calling but Ellen went to seminary to receive hers." It was there at Asbury Theological Seminary in Wilmore, Kentucky, that God fanned into flame the gift of teaching His Word into Ellen. I am proud to say I am Ellen's husband. I am blessed that she has been obedient to God's call on her life to teach His Word. And along the way she has taught this man, her husband.

The words of her book are truth. As I read it for the first time, I cried over and over; I laughed again and again. I was encouraged over and over; again and again. I revisited her crisis because it was really *our* crisis.

God was at work in Ellen to author this book and she did not even know it. Close to the beginning of her crisis she began informing others of her journey through the website, carepages.com. Unknown to her at the time, she was writing the outline of this book. Even then she was encouraging people who were wondering how they could be a source of encouragement to her.

It is now almost five years since *that day* and God is still getting glory for what He has done and is doing in her life.

She did not fall to pieces in her crisis then and she hasn't now.

Crises, we all have them. Crises are never scheduled. They catch us off guard. No one can know when a crisis is coming, but we can be prepared for it when it does. This book does prepare us for crisis and reminds us that there is a danger but also an opportunity present.

The danger is clear: a crisis could cause us to fall apart. Too many fall into this danger.

A crisis can also be an opportunity. Instead of falling to pieces, we can find great promise and possibility before, during, and after the crisis. I hope that anyone reading this book will use it as a means to allow your crisis to be an opportunity.

My prayer is that Ellen's story, this book, causes you to think and be stirred to conversation with God, with another person, or even in a small group setting. This book has the potential to be used powerfully through intentional conversation. Therefore, I offer the following study questions pertaining to each chapter as a guide to help begin intentional conversation or for your own personal reflection.

This book uses Proverbs 24:10 as its theme. Allow this prayer, formed around this verse, to help as you get started.

> *Father, Your Word confronts and challenges me. You say that if I fall to pieces in a crisis, then there wasn't much to me in the first place. I am in a crisis now or I recognize I could be in one in the near future. As I experience whatever the crisis is, will You help me? Help me to not fall to pieces. Help me to be prepared for it. Help me to ponder it and not be pounded by it. Help me to see I am not alone. You are with me and so are the people in my life that you have surrounded me with. Help me to be persistent in moving forward and not giving up. Give me Your power and Your peace so that in the midst of my crisis I can prevail. You said I would have trouble in this world but that I could overcome that trouble. I don't want to simply survive my crisis; I want to be victorious. I don't want to fall to pieces in my crisis; I want the peace of Christ to prevail. Thank you for the provision of Jesus who makes all this possible. In His name I pray, Amen!*

Study Questions

chapter 1

Prior to the Crisis

Ellen woke up one morning and everything changed.

What experience have you gone through, or are you going through, that changed everything?

What was your situation in life at that time? What life events were going on around you?

What was your initial response? In other words, did you start to fall to pieces or was something else happening?

Were you spiritually prepared for what you were going through or what changes do you need to make to be ready?

chapter 2
Preparation Before the Crisis

Ellen wrote, *For a Christian, a believer, who desires to focus on the preparation before the crisis, this is a crucial point…Know ahead of time that nothing stands in the way of your growth in your relationship with Jesus; not even a crisis. The right time to draw your line is before the crisis comes and say, "No matter what, I will not fall to pieces."*

How can "drawing your line" help you in preparing for a crisis?

Where do you stand? Is there a crisis that you have said, "If this happened I would fall to pieces?"

How does your relationship to God have everything to do with crisis?

S.L.O.W. living takes the focus off of self and onto God.

Could you identify with Ellen's mantra? What benefits or consequences would come if you committed or didn't commit to S.L.O.W. living?

chapter 3
Pondering the Crisis

Two realistic responses to a crisis are *ponder or panic.*

Do you normally respond by pondering? Or panicking?

Ponder in Greek language is the word *sumballo,* which literally means *to bring together in one's mind, to confer with one's self.*

How can a commitment to ponder prevent panic?

What other benefits can come from pondering a crisis? What consequences come from panic?

Psalm 16:5 (NIV) "Lord, You have *assigned* me my portion and my cup..."

How does the thought that your crisis is an assignment by God help you to ponder your crisis?

chapter 4

People Surrounding the Crisis

Ellen says that surrounding yourself with the right people, allowing the right people in the center of your bull's eye, is critical when you're faced with a crisis.

Who are the people you have surrounded yourself with? How do they help or hinder you in a crisis?

In the midst of crisis are you the type of person who allows people in or pushes them away? What are the benefits and consequences to each?

How have the people in your life "surprised" you? What gifts of agape helped you?

Draw a target with three rings. Consider the friends in your life. Begin placing them where they fit best on your bull's eye. In the center, write the names of your closest friends, those who push you to be better and are always surrounding you. (Remember this place only has room for a few people.) Now add the names of your other friends in the middle and outer rings.

Thank God for those people in the center of your bull's eye. Consider writing them a text, and email, or call them and let them know how blessed you are to have them surrounding you in your crises.

chapter 5
Persistence Through the Crisis

Strong-willed was defined as: stubborn, resolute, and obstinate (see definitions.)

Are you strong-willed?

How can being strong-willed aid in "not falling to pieces in a crisis?"

Jochebed is a Biblical example of a strong willed person who didn't fall to pieces in her crisis.

How did her story inspire you?

Who is your example, Biblical or other, of a strong willed person?
How have they inspired you?

A strong willed person is *one who is firmly & stubbornly determined to maintain a purpose* through persistence.

Are you determined to be strong-willed?

What needs to change within you, your relationship with God, to become this person?

chapter 6
Provision Through the Crisis

Manna is an unexpected help or aid. Manna is provision from God.

How has God provided manna in your life in times of crisis?

Have you ever been close to falling to pieces in a crisis when manna came?

What is it?

Have you ever fallen to pieces in a crisis but a fresh supply of manna delivered you from falling further? What was it?

chapter 7
Power Over the Crisis

Mark chapter five introduces you to a woman with an issue.

What is your issue (crisis)?

Does your crisis have power over you? If this is the case, what needs to change?

A crisis can drive us crazy or drive us to the Christ.

Is your crisis driving you crazy? Is your crisis driving you to Christ?

Do you have a relationship with Christ? Is he Savior of your life? If not, are you ready to begin?

How is Christ freeing you from your crisis?

How has Christ made you, or making you, whole in your crisis?

Someone is always paying attention to you, whether you're in crisis or not.

Is this comforting or convicting?

How does knowing Christ has His eyes on you help you?

How does realizing that a crowd is watching you affect you?

chapter 8
Peace vs. Piece in the Crisis

Crisis can cause us to fall to pieces or experience the Peace of Christ. Praising the Lord in every situation can go a long way to knowing His peace.

Do you normally "praise the Lord" or "blame the Lord" in a crisis?

Do the people around you help you praise God or blame God? Do you need to make different choices in the people closest to you in order for them to encourage you to praise more?

Many people can survive a crisis. Fewer find victory over their crisis.

Are you surviving or are you victorious over your crisis?

In what ways are you simply surviving?

In what ways are you victorious?

chapter 9

Possibility & Promise after the Crisis

Ellen writes: *As I step back and look at this incredible journey as one big puzzle I am taken aback, surprised, humbled, amazed, jaw-dropped, excited, giddy, jubilant, about-ready-to-squeal, at the ways my Lord maneuvered His Hand prior to my crisis, during my crisis and after the crisis.* She then proceeded to talk more about her adoption process.

How has God worked in your life after your crisis?

Many times we are simply glad to get through the crisis that we fail to ponder after it.
Take some time to write down the many ways God has moved in your life.

How are you a different person? How are you a better person? Are you bitter toward your crisis?

Ellen used her crisis to proclaim Christ in many ways.

How are you proclaiming to others what Christ did for you in the midst of your crisis? How might it inspire others?

Proverbs 24:10 (The Message) says, "If you fall to pieces in a crisis there wasn't much to you in the first place."

How do you feel about this verse?

How has this book helped you?

Write Ellen and let her know how this book has helped you. Who knows how your story might encourage her when her next crisis hits? Email Ellen at slowlivinlady@gmail.com.
You can also visit her website at www.slowlivin.com.

CPSIA information can be obtained at www.ICGtesting.com
Printed in the USA
LVOW08s0822251114

415364LV00034BA/2384/P

9 781490 842479